# TRITON'S TREASURE

Steps to Christ for Kids

by

# Sally Streib

## Sea n' See Presentations

Teaching kids of all ages to know and love
their God.

www.seansee.net

SEAWAY BOOKS

Cover art by Marcus Mashburn
Cover and book design by David Valentin.
Photographs Copyright by Sally Streib, David
Valentin, and Reggie Thomas

Bible verses quoted are used by permission from
The Clear Word.
Copyright © 1994 by Jack J. Blanco

These stories are all true and the people are real.

AIMHIGHER
AVID INK MEDIA

Seaway Books are published by Avid Ink Media,
a division of Big Idea Development Center, LLC
Encinitas California

Also By
Sally Streib

**Kids Books**

Treasures by the Sea, Book 1

Treasures By the Sea Workbook:
27 Bible Truths for Kids

Summer of the Sharks, Book 2

Summer of the Sharks Workbook

Octopus Encounter, Book 3

Octopus Encounter DVD 1 and 2

Intruder Alert!, Book 4

The Girl God Rescued

God's Fantastic Sea Creatures:
Coloring and Story Book

**Adult Books**

The Heart Mender

## Dedication

This book is dedicated to Jesus. He created the wonderful sea creatures in these stories, and tucked a truth about Himself into each one. Then He sent me off to leap into the ocean and discover them one by one. Next He said, "Go tell others," and this has been the great joy of my life for over thirty years. Thank you, Jesus!

# A Note From the Author

One morning, while reading the beloved little book, STEPS TO CHRIST, I said to myself, "Why can't kids get the same wonderful help as adults have received from this book. They can learn while still young. They are smart.

I gathered twenty of my sea experiences and put them together with God's Word to help kids learn the same great truths as my favorite book. I wrote, TRITON'S TREASURES, using the two things I know best as a Christian and a SCUBA diver- God's Word and His sea creatures.

We always remember best the things we touch, hear, taste, see, and smell, so experiences in nature reach right down into our souls and teach us about the Creator. He gave us His Word to help us understand what He and His creation is trying to teach us.

There are steps that God takes us through as we come to know Him, choose Him and walk with Him. Each of the ten sections, with two stories each, will show you a step you can take. Becoming a friend of God will be the greatest adventure of your life. Enjoy!

Sally Streib

# Contents

# Part 1

## Help! I'm in Trouble

*Our Need of a Savior*

Pacific Ocean waves.

# Chapter 1
## Swallowed by a Wave

This is the spot," I said to my three kids, Sally, Steve, and David. "Let's set up our picnic on that small beach down there." I pointed to a narrow stretch of sand a hundred feet below us that was already scattered with families, sunbathers, and surfers waxing their boards.

As I gazed out over the rolling Pacific Ocean, bright in the late morning sunlight, I remembered the warm summer days years ago when my Aunt Ann and I would hop in her little red Renault sports car and drive over the hills in Riverside, California, to Laguna Beach. While Aunt Ann relaxed on a lounge chair, I would spend the day riding the ocean swells, body surfing on giant green waves, and exploring the tide pools that nestled among the rocks at the foot of the cliffs.

I loved the sea and had recently taken SCUBA lessons so I could get a closer look at its wonders. Now I wanted to share all this with my grown kids.

"How will we get down there, Mom?" Sally asked, joining me at the edge of the cliff and peering over at the waves that crashed against the rocks.

"There's a path somewhere near here," I replied, poking among the tall grass that grew to the edge of the cliffs.

My kids followed, stepping through a patchwork quilt of purple lupine flowers and golden California poppies.

"Here's the trail," I cried over the sound of the surf. "Let's go!"

We picked up our beach bags and lunch basket, then carefully made our way down the rugged trail that wound its way through the scrub brush like a sea snake swirling through a coral reef. When we reached the end of the trail, we jumped the last two feet onto the beach.

It had been over ten years since I had seen my beloved Pacific Ocean. The instant my feet hit the beach I dropped the bag of towels, collecting bags and field guides. I sat down and kicked off my shoes, digging my feet into the sun-warmed California sand.

"Where do you want to put the blanket, Mom?" Steve asked.

"There's a good spot past the lifeguard tower," David answered for me.

"That looks perfect," I said. "It's not too crowded."

The ocean's waves called out to me. "Come on, Sally. Dive in," they shouted. I jumped up and headed for the water.

"Get the lunch out," I called, handing David my beach bag and shoes. "I'll be right back."

I jogged along the beach past the lifeguard tower. I noticed a sign nailed to the tower that listed

*4*

ocean safety tips. *Maybe I should take a moment to glance over the rules or ask the Lifeguard about surf conditions before I dash into the water,* I thought, but I just couldn't wait to feel the power of the surf swirl around me.

I splashed through the shallow water toward the line of breakers and plunged in, shivering at the touch of the cold water.

Coming up for air, I stared at the huge waves crashing in front of me. *I don't remember them being this big,* I thought. I felt a sudden rush of fear wash over me, but kept on moving farther away from the shore, knowing that I had to get to the first wave before it fell over on itself and me. My hands clawed through the water, catching bits of seaweed in my fingers as I swam closer and closer to the breaking waves. Then I burst through the surface again and stood up.

"Wow!" I cried.

In front of me a giant wall of green rose up over my head and filled the sky. The wave wore a white wig of foam. Suddenly the wind caught the foam and flung it into the air, scattering it. A glop splattered across my face.

Dive fast! Dive deep! My mind screamed, remembering what my SCUBA instructor taught me. "If you get caught in a line of breakers, don't panic. Don't try to run for shore. Dive down into the bottom of the wave. The water beneath a wave is calm."

Nothing about that monster wave looked calm.

*I'm about to die. I've got to get to shore. I'm going to drown out here. My kids will never know what happened to me.* Panicky thoughts raced through my mind.

5

I hesitated for another moment.

The wave fell on top of me and swallowed me up like an angry sea monster. I dove in. *Too late,* I thought.

The giant wave poured its salty froth into my mouth. It picked sand up from the bottom and pounded it into my hair. It tugged at my arms and legs, tumbling me over and over. Finally, as if deciding I didn't taste good after all, the wave spat me out onto the beach.

I lay in shallow water gulping fresh air. Sea foam and seaweed swirled around me. I tried to stand, but the retreating water tugged at my legs, trying to pull me back down the slope of the beach and into the sea beyond.

Up on the dry sand, two men laughed as they threw a Frisbee back and forth. Three children giggled, patting the wet walls of a sand castle. Next to the lifeguard tower, two women lounged on folding chairs hiding behind dark glasses and glamor magazines.

No one noticed me. They didn't see my struggle. I could almost reach out and touch the safe shore, but my body refused to stand up and run.

Behind me I heard another wave thunder against the sand.

"Run," my brain screamed, but my muscles refused to move. I tried to stand, but my legs buckled. I crumpled onto the wet sand as another wave roared over me, grabbing and throwing me around like a weightless beach ball. It thumped my face across the sea bottom as a boy pounds a basketball across the court. It flipped me over and drove the last precious ounces of air from my lungs. Then it swirled me around and around like a wet beach towel in a clothes dryer. It finally retreated to the deep sea, leaving me in a heap unable to move.

"Need help?" a man's voice called from the shore.

I wiped the sand from my eyes and looked up at a young man wearing blue shorts and a baseball cap standing not far away on the beach.

Hope sprang into my heart. "Help," I wanted to scream. "I'm in big trouble." Then, for one foolish moment, I hesitated.

*Wait a minute,* I thought. *I'm a SCUBA diver. I've dived into half the seas around the world. I don't need help. The shore is so close.*

I looked up at a cluster of people gathering on the beach. Someone pointed in my direction.

*I have to show these people that I'm not afraid,* I thought.

Then I heard a third wave roaring toward the place where I lay like a heap of seaweed. This time, I didn't hesitate. "Help," I sputtered.

"Hold on. The lifeguard is coming," the young man shouted as he splashed into the shallow water waving his cap.

I looked down the beach and saw a bronzed lifeguard scanning the sea with a pair of binoculars. He spotted me and leaped down from the platform. I could see his leg muscles flexing and heard his feet splash in the shallow water as he ran toward me. He looked wonderful. The wind caught strands of blond hair and whipped it about. I lay breathless, waiting.

Every eye in the crowd followed the lifeguard as he ran along the wet sand, a red torpedo buoy stashed under one arm. They craned their necks and peered through their sunglasses. Seconds later the lifeguard arrived. He swept me up in his strong arms before another wave could grab me, and carried me to the safety of the warm, dry sand.

The crowd clapped. They clapped because the lifeguard had heard my cry for help and saved me. They cheered because I had put aside my pride and chose to ask for help.

Someone brought a warm beach towel and draped it around my shaking shoulders. The lifeguard poured a bottle of water over my face and hair.

"We need to keep all the sand, here on the beach," he laughed.

I sighed. For a few frantic minutes I had felt completely helpless. Now, safely on the dry beach, I felt totally safe, far from the reach of the powerful waves. *I understand the importance of swimming within sight of the lifeguard,* I thought.

"Can somebody get my family?" I gasped. "Look for three teens just beyond the tower." The young man in blue shorts trotted away. A few minutes later he came running back with my kids in tow.

"Are you alright?" David and Steve asked together.

"Mom. What are you doing? This is so embarrassing," my daughter said, looking around on the crowd that began to disperse.

"Thank you," she said, finally noticing the handsome lifeguard.

We trudged off down the beach to our picnic spot. No lunch ever tasted so good and no sunshine ever warmed me as pleasantly as that sunshine.

The hurdles you're jumping in your life might not be giant Pacific waves. When you face overwhelming trouble and begin to hear the sounds of disaster charging toward you, stop. Listen! You will hear a voice calling out, "Do you need help?"

Don't hesitate. Don't think, "I've handled many things worse than this. I know what I'm doing." Just cry out, "I need help."

Jesus is like a strong and handsome lifeguard sitting in his tower. His eyes carefully scan the world, looking for those in trouble. He knows that life is sometimes like a raging sea. Wave after wave of difficulty can sweep over you. One minute you're laughing as you leap over the sea mounds, and the next second a wild rogue wave slams into you. Just as rough water can tear the strength right out of you, life's unexpected troubles can rip hope out of your heart. He knows this because He lived here. He rode the swells of trouble and surfed the waves of difficulty.

God rescued Him many times. Satan tried to kill Him in Bethlehem before He even learned to walk. God saved Him and sent Him to Egypt by night. When He visited His hometown in Nazareth, a maddened crowd tried to shove Him over a cliff, and God hid Him until he could walk away, unseen. Angry men stood bunched together, watching Him heal the sick. They plotted His death. This is why He knows how to rescue you.

There are three wonderful things about your lifeguard that you need to know.

Jesus is all-powerful. He created the entire universe by speaking a few words. He uses this power to help people in trouble. The Bible tells us how His power made a lead ax head float when a boy prayed for help. When He commanded it, the Red Sea split apart, leaving a dry pathway so His trapped people could escape their Egyptian enemies. An empty grain sack and oil bottle refilled, time after time, when a hungry mother prayed for food to feed her son. His amazing power even made a dead man walk out of a tomb alive.

The second wonderful fact to consider is that

Jesus IS love. He doesn't just do loving things, He IS LOVE. This love is perfect and lasts forever. It's the reason for all He does. No one can destroy it nor change it.

Jesus lived to help us understand God's love for us. When Jesus walked in this dark world, He let God's love burst from Him in every kind thing He did. He even allowed Himself to be nailed to a cross so that He could rescue you give you the gift of life. That's LOVE!

The third truth about Jesus that should give you great confidence in Him is that He knows everything. He has all the information that exists. He has the wisdom to use all this information to choose the best way to help you.

There is nothing about you that He doesn't know. He gets it. He knows how you feel. He knows your motives and your longings. He has a deep interest in them all. He also knows what to do about them and because He loves you and has the power to do something, He will.

So, when you face a wild, thrashing sea, you can depend upon His love, His power, and His knowledge. He will rescue you and set your feet on solid ground, wrapped in a warm blanket of His love.

When I dive into the calm, sparkling waters of the Bahamas and the South Pacific, I learn exciting lessons from the resident creatures. And in the deep seas of Hawaii and Mexico, God sends crabs, fish, and seashells to help me know Him.

If you're up for adventure, come on. Let's plunge beneath the surface of the sea where the water is calm. Dive deep. Let's learn more about the Great Lifeguard from the sea creatures.

You've read your Bible; now prepare yourself for

a different adventure. God's sea creatures want to teach you many things. If you're ready, dive now! Dive deep!

## Discussion Questions

- What are some of the ways Jesus shows us how much he loves us?
- Name the three truths about Jesus that give us confidence in Him.

## Chapter 2
# Shark!

**M**y dive buddy, Martha, and I climbed aboard the dive boat as it lay tied to the dock sloshing up and down in the mild ocean swell.

It seemed like only a few days ago that we had completed six weeks of SCUBA diving classes. We listened to our dive instructor's lessons, watched videos, and practiced every SCUBA skill in the local swimming pool. For hours, we poured over dozens of books before choosing the best dive equipment and placing our order. After the gear arrived, we tried everything on, laughing at our strange forms in the mirror.

As soon as our class was over, we packed up our gear and swimwear and drove south. At the far end of Florida, we looked out over the small islands that lay like a string of pearls flung out over the azure water.

Soon eight other new divers, who had also passed the written test, joined us. We felt ready to demonstrate dive skills in the real ocean.

Our dive master, John, untied the ropes that held the boat to the dock and revved up the motor. We sped over the blue water, heading for Horseshoe reef. "The shallow reef sits about four miles from the dock at Marathon Key," John said. "You'll be able to see it when we get a bit closer."

"The first thing I want to see is a huge brain coral," a girl wearing a bright yellow dive suit said. "I've seen pictures of some that are bigger than sea turtles."

"The first thing I don't want to see is a shark," I groaned, rolling my eyes.

"You'd be lucky to see one shark in a lifetime of diving," John replied.

"Good," Martha said.

"If I see one," a boy, struggling into his dive boots, said, "I'll ram my tank into his mouth before he can bite me."

"I'll just freeze in place," the girl next to him said, standing up and jamming her arms against her sides.

*I'll be so busy keeping track of all my weird gear that I won't even know one is near,* I thought.

The captain dropped anchor just beyond the reef to avoid damaging any coral. All of us suited up. Now it was time to jump into the sea and become real divers.

"When I tell you to leap, stick your right foot out and take a giant step off the end of the boat," John, explained. "The sea is a bit rough today. The boat will rise up on a swell, pausing for only a second before plunging into a trough. That's when you leap. The boat will be almost level. Don't hesitate."

I nodded. The dive master knew what to do and when to do it. I planned to obey his instructions to the last detail. As the boat rose up over a swell and prepared to dip into the trough, I prayed that John would tell me to leap before I simply fell off the end of the boat or a great swell reached up and snatched me from my perch.

At his command, I stuck my right foot forward and plunged in. Splash! I felt my body hit the water and close over my head. Immediately I kicked my fins and surfaced, raising my hand to form a circle with my right thumb and forefinger. This OK signal told my dive buddy, Martha, that my gear still clung to my body, my mask stuck tight, and she could leap into the water beside me.

"Jump!" I heard the dive master scream, again. I saw a flash of hesitation in Martha's eyes, but she thrust her right foot forward and left the safety of the dive platform behind. I bobbed about, watching as she hit the water and disappeared from sight.

Soon she surfaced and checked her gear, giving me the OK sign. We pinched our noses and blew gently. This cleared our ears as we slowly sank to the bottom of the sea. The water was calm thirty feet beneath the surface. We leveled out just above the sand, checked our dive computers, and moved away from the boat. John swam behind us.

I laughed, thinking how I must look to a fish, with a regulator jammed into my mouth, a tank strapped to my back, and a mask clamped over my face. It felt strange having a knife attached to my leg, lead weights wrapped around my waist, and two long fins sticking from the ends of my feet. My gloved hands clutched a dive light, a collecting bag, and a dive computer that gave all sorts of information.

In spite of the bulky equipment and fears about my ability to use each piece, I felt excited. *Now I can swim with the fish,* I thought. *I can discover treasures hidden in the reef.*

I followed a Rainbow Parrotfish around a large Star Coral and watched an Arrow Crab prance on legs not much thicker than a human hair.

My dive buddy pointed out a Peacock Flounder that oozed along the sand. Two eyes sat on one side of his flat head and each turned in a different direction at the same time. I wanted to laugh, but my mouth clung to my regulator instead.

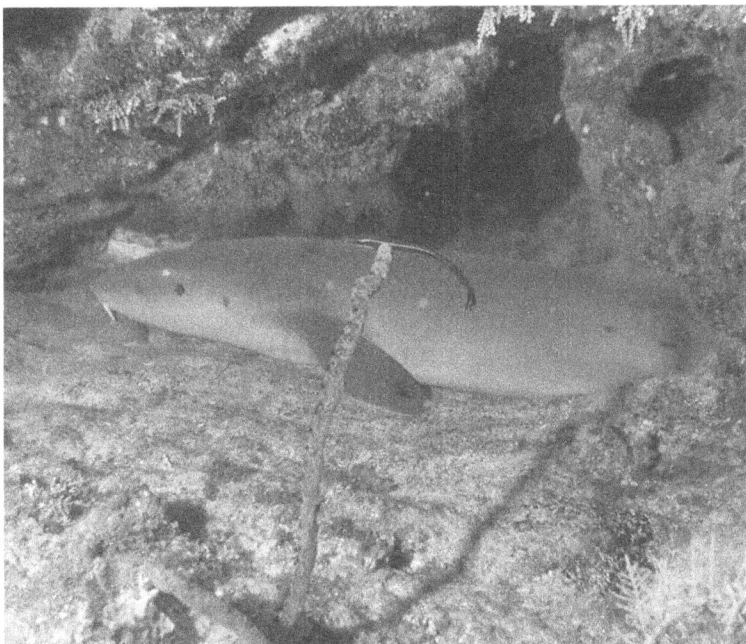

A Nurse Shark lurks in the shadows.

We headed across the shallow lagoon to the reef crest. Suddenly I spied a brown and white shell sticking out from a narrow ledge. Grabbing it, I ran my fingers along its smooth shell. The snail-like creature pulled itself inside and snapped the opening shut with a hard fingernail called the operculum.

*I'll take this to the boat where I can get a closer look,* I thought; opening my collecting bag.

Before I could drop the shell into the bag, the animal thrust its operculum at me, scratching my finger. I managed to scream and still hold on to my air supply, but I flung the shell away. Blood dripped into the water. I pinched the cut between my fingers to stop the bleeding, then dove down and picked up the shell. It stuck out the thin operculum and swayed it back and forth trying to locate my fingers again.

*That's a sharp tool,* I thought, watching the shell pull its foot inside and slam the front door. This creature's behavior surprised me. *I wonder what other weird behavior I might see as I discover other creatures that live around the reef,* I thought, tucking the shell back into a tiny cave.

I glanced up to check on the location of my dive buddy. Suddenly I saw a great mouth coming toward me. I stared at the sleek form that followed the gaping mouth. Sharp triangular teeth stuck up and down all over the place. The edges of the teeth looked like miniature saw blades.

"Shark!" I screamed into my regulator. *You're dripping blood, my brain screamed. Sharks can smell a drop of blood in thousands of gallons of water. You're in big trouble. Get back to the boat.*

"Don't move toward the surface too fast," the dive master had told us. "Count out about a foot a second." But, right now, who was counting

"Don't take too many big strokes with those new giant fins," my dive master had warned when I leaped off the boat moments earlier. Your muscles aren't ready for that and you could get a..."

I hadn't heard the rest of his warning because the

water closed over me, drowning out his words.

The sight of that shark made me flip my fins so hard my calf muscle cramped. "Ouch!" I groaned doubling up. *That's what John was trying to tell me.*

Suddenly I remembered what I should do if I got a cramp. I straightened my leg and grabbed the end of the fin, pulling it toward my stomach.

*This really works,* I thought. The cramp eased and I remembered the shark. I took off toward the boat as fast as I dared, slashing the water with my hands and kicking my fins. I reached out and grabbed the handrail on the dive ladder and climbed right onto it without taking my fins off.

"Don't try to climb the boat ladder until you remove your fins. Wait for someone in the boat to take them from you," John's words rang out in my mind. But, who was waiting?

I started climbing the ladder when something grasped my left fin. "I'm dead," I gasped, spitting out my mouthpiece. T*hat shark has grabbed me by the fin even though I'm half out of the water,* I thought. I cringed, expecting to hear the crunching of broken bones and feel my flesh being torn from my body.

Two seconds later, I realized that I was still alive, I glanced over my shoulder. Martha clutched my left fin with both hands. Relief flooded through me. A shark didn't have me in its jaws. "What are you trying to do?" I shouted, unable to ascend the ladder any further.

"Why did you take off like that?" she screamed, her eyes wide inside her mask. "Why are you going up the ladder with your fins still on?"

I thrust my right arm straight ahead and clamped my hand into a fist, remembering the diver's signal for DANGER. She glanced about, still hanging on to my fin. "I don't see anything," she said.

"Shark!" I yelled through my mouthpiece. The word came out mumbled and deformed, but she heard it. Her eyes almost popped off her face and into her mask. She released me, and sprang at the ladder with both hands, slashing the water with her fins. I stared at her calf muscles. They bulged as she pumped her legs and made wild gyrations in the water. She slammed both fins onto the lower ladder rung, clamoring up right past me.

I hurried up the ladder behind Martha and fell on top of her where she lay on the bottom of the boat, breathing hard. We both spit out our regulators.

The boat captain burst out in a paroxysm of laughter. He reached over and lifted us both up. We settled onto a seat and removed our fins.

Suddenly John pierced the surface of the water just beyond the boat. He spit out his mouthpiece. "Hey, what's going on?" You both have another 30 minutes before you have to be out of the water."

"I saw a...shark!" I said, as if that should explain the whole thing.

John didn't laugh, but he struggled to swallow a smile that threatened to spread across his face. "Yes," he said. He pressed his lips together tight. He looked away for a moment. "There are sometimes sharks out there," he said, looking at the captain who was doubled over in unrestrained laughter.

"And other stuff," Martha said, ignoring the captain.

"Let's go over the rules I taught you that help you avoid panic," John suggested, "Stay together and watch out for each other. If you see a shark, stay calm and move slowly out of his territory. Never thrash around. That will just attract his attention. And, don't try to out-swim him because you can't."

"Oh!" we both said together, looking at each other.

"Now get back in here," he urged.

*We'll never dive again if we don't do it now,* I thought, sticking my mouthpiece back into my mouth.

"Don't worry about that shark. He's long gone," John assured us.

We jammed on our fins and leaped off the boat. Our bodies sank a few feet, then we surfaced.

"Don't worry," John said. "Stay with me. I'm not afraid of sharks."

I pointed my head down and let myself sink to the white sand below. A beautiful five-pointed creature stared up at me. Martha joined me and we spent several minutes examining the huge sea star.

I ran my fingers over the lumpy back. *I guess that's why nothing ever sticks to sea stars,* I thought. These tiny bumps don't leave any room for creatures to attach themselves to them.

We placed the sea star back onto the sand and sped away. The next 30 minutes passed quickly. Every few minutes I cast a quick glance behind me, wondering if the shark still cruised the reef or lay watching me from a safe distance. I saw Martha check once or twice to see if John swam nearby. But at last, God's other sea creatures captured our attention.

We soon forgot about all the scary things that might lurk about. *True, the water holds its terrors,* I thought, *but we have faced our fears and we've learned to trust the dive master. I don't think either of us will panic again.*

For the next three days, we zigzagged across quiet bays and followed the edges of scattered coral reefs.

## Shark!

If that shark and its friends cruised the water near us, we didn't see them. We kept our focus on all the beautiful creatures in the reef.

After diving Molasses reef and Pickle reef and demonstrating our dive skills, John handed us our new PADI dive cards. We officially joined the family of those who could skillfully enter the sea and come out alive.

Maybe you love life like I love diving. You want to cruise and discover and enjoy, but you know that Satan, like an old shark, lurks nearby. You've seen how his lies and temptations have ripped and torn your life and the lives of family and friends. You know you're no match for this enemy even as I knew I couldn't save myself from that shark if it decided to attack.

Don't panic, even when you know you're in big trouble. Your great Dive Master is nearby. God sent Jesus to die for you and be with you always. Jesus lived here in shark-infested waters. He knows what it's like for you. Satan gave Him a lot of trouble, even using wicked people to nail Him to a cross. Sin, that He didn't commit, broke His heart. But it gave Him the right to forgive you and be nearby as you journey through the reef of life.

Jesus is the perfect shark repellent. When you need him in times of temptation or in fear, just say, "Help! I'm in big trouble. I need you, Jesus". And, Jesus, who isn't afraid of Satan, will guide you and help you.

## Discussion Questions

- Why do you think I chose to get back into the water in spite of the presence of sharks?
- What does it mean to Panic?
- Why is panicking not a good way to face danger?
- Why do you think Jesus isn't afraid of Satan? Why is this important to you?

# Part 2

## Is Anybody Out There?

### Understanding the Gospel

The coral reef is home to many of God's sea creatures.

## Chapter 3
# *Miracle Rescue*

I stood looking down on Honaunau Bay, a shallow body of water that wraps around the foot of a mountain on the edge of Oahu, Hawaii's main island. The bay shimmered in the noonday sun. I walked down a trail and stopped at the water's edge. I put my mask in place and lowered the strap over the back of my head. As I sat down to fit my fins over my dive boots, a gull flew past and squawked at me. It watched as I strapped my knife scabbard to my leg.

"You're going to love it in there," a strange voice said.

I looked up. A young boy in blue swim trunks stood in the sea in front of me. He stepped out of the water. A large puddle formed at his feet. He shoved his mask back onto his forehead, pushing a large fringe of red hair up behind it. He swiped his hand across his freckled face, wiping off water and flashing me a grin that rivaled the sun.

"I saw the Humuhumu-nukunuku-a-pua'a out

24

there," he said.

"You saw what?" I said, jumping to my feet.

"It's a triggerfish," he answered. "It makes a little grunting pig-like sound. It also has a needle-like spine on its back. That's how he got the name, Humuhumu-nukunuku-a-pua'a.

"That's quite a name," I said, grinning.

"It means, fish that sews and grunts like a pig. This is a picture of it." He held up a plastic card with a dozen fish printed on it.

"You certainly know your fish," I said, taking the card in my hands and studying the pictures.

"You'll see fish all over the place out there." He laughed, his eyes dancing with delight. "Be sure to snorkel around that overhang," he said, pointing to the right side of the bay. "I saw a little cave and it's full of small fish. I think that's where they hide from predators."

"Thanks for the tips," I replied, turning and backing into the water. I moved slowly so I wouldn't trip over my new power fins.

He watched me, an inner joy bursting out through his eyes. "Hey," he added, "Watch out for that whirlpool. It's off to the far right at the mouth of the bay."

*Wow!* I thought as I dipped below the surface of the bay. *I can see more than 100 feet ahead. That's good visibility. I'm in paradise.*

Rainbow-colored fish swished past me as I glided along. A gold and black Morish Idol darted by as if following its own long snout, and a Fantail Filefish with velvety skin twitched its tail like I often fan my face when sitting in the tropical sun. A silver barracuda moved along beside me, staring. He shadowed me for ten minutes before gliding off into the distance.

I watched color-splashed angelfish flit about decorating the bay and smiled at a shy Black Banded Wrasse with weird buckteeth. It peeked from its hiding place among the corals. A giggle burst from my throat and into my snorkel.

*I want to come here every day for the rest of my life,* I thought to myself. *I want to jump into this bay, kick my fins, and follow the fish as they dart about. I want to laugh at the fat puffers and enjoy the colors of the butterflyfish.*

When a Whitespot Goatfish swam into view, I gulped air, held my breath, and dove. I followed him as he probed the sand for food using a pair of feelers called barbels that hung to each side of its face. Finally, my empty lungs forced me to return to the surface.

For three wonderful days I swam all over the bay, pressing further and further out to the open sea each time. I learned that I could expect to find some fish in the same place each day. They seemed to swim in territories and never ventured far beyond an invisible line in the sea. Crevice-dwelling creatures defended their places in the reef from other creatures that passed too close.

Small fish darted in and out among the waving tentacles of sea anemones. Crabs picked up little anemones and carried them around on their backs because they knew the stings of the anemones would scare off predators. Hermit crabs snatched up empty shells and toted them about, popping inside at a moment's notice when an enemy approached.

By the fourth day I felt like the creatures were my friends. I made the rounds laughing at them and saying, "Good morning." The hours passed quickly, but at last, I headed toward shallow water. *I just have to rest and warm up,* I thought. When I stood up, I noticed several people removing their masks and heading for shore.

"What's up?" I called to a man nearby.

"We've just been told that a bad storm is coming this way. It looks like a possible hurricane and they want everyone out of the water."

I looked into the sky. A mass of black clouds moved toward the bay, unrolling and spreading itself out like a blanket.

"Going to be a big one," the man said, removing his fins. "I'm getting out of this water."

I just stood there looking out over the sea. I imagined that soon the clouds would shut out the sun and the wind whip up the sea, sending waves slamming against the shore. I imagined the tiny fish being flung onto the beach where they would gasp for air, beat their fins against sand, and die.

*Without the fish, the bay will be ruined,* I thought, remembering shallow bays in the Bahamas where great storms had churned up the sea, cast small fish to shore, and toppled corals. *I can't just stand here and let my friends flit about until they're caught and destroyed by the storm,* I thought.

"I'm going to warn those fish," I shouted, not caring that people leaving the water stared at me. I dove into the water and yelled through my snorkel at the fish and crabs. "Dive deep into the bay or hide in the cave by the big rock," I screamed. You'll be safe from the hurricane that's coming." I moved into deeper water and yelled some more.

A butterfly fish darted past my feet. Crabs crawled over the small rocks on the sea bottom. A school of Sailfin Tangs swished by. They paid no attention to me.

I screamed in frustration. "Hide deep in the sea. A storm is coming. If you dive deep, the rough water will pass over you."

Not one crab darted into a crevice. No fish hid behind coral branches. Not a single creature noticed the water darkening as the covering of black clouds rolled over the sky above the bay.

Suddenly I realized that I knew the danger, but I couldn't warn the fish because I didn't know one word of fish language. They couldn't understand me and didn't see me as a friend that they should pay any attention to. I felt helpless. A universe separated me from the fish I loved. When they looked at me all they saw was a strange visitor to their world. They did not know I wanted to save them.

I realized, with a sudden jolt, that the only way to help them would be to become one of them. I'd have to sprout fins, grow a tail, develop gills, and learn to dart among the corals. I'd have to learn their language, swim in fish schools, and slither into coral crevices like the shy wrasses. I'd even have to wiggle beneath the sand with the flounders. If I could do all this, they might listen to me. Then they would let me guide them to deep places for safety.

But becoming a fish would take a miracle. Becoming a fish would be dangerous. A shark might catch me and tear me to pieces, or a Tiger Moray could slash me with its needle-like teeth. Becoming a fish could cost me my life.

I stood up, removed my fins and sloshed toward shore. "Dear God, you made those fish. Please look after them." I prayed.

Later that day I sat curled up in my warm bungalow as the rain pounded the window and the wind whirled through the palm trees. I thought about my tiny friends in the cold, churning water.

"That's it," I shouted, jumping to my feet. "That's how you felt, God, when you saw the storm of sin heading for the world full of beautiful people that you created and called your friends. It must have been terrible. You knew sin would kill them if you didn't do something to help. You couldn't save them from afar. So, you sent your Son to became one of them. He lived and worked and hurt with them."

Think about what happened to me in Honaunau Bay. It shows you two important things. First, you really are in big trouble, and second, there really is someone out there who cares. His name is God.

The God who loves you says, "I was ready to show myself to those who didn't ask for me. I was ready to be found by those who didn't look for me. I said, 'Here I am, here I am...'" Isaiah 65:1

He wants you to know He's out there. He wants you to know His story. He longs for you to look at Him and discover the One who loves you.

You can read about what God did to solve the sin problem in Genesis, the first book of the Bible. This book tells you how Adam and Eve, the first people God created, sinned. They got into big trouble. God looked down at their storm-tossed world. He said, "I'm going to send my precious Son, Jesus, down there. My friends are in trouble."

Because Jesus came, you can "see" what God is like by reading the stories that tell you how Jesus lived and how He treated people. You can understand Him through the lessons He put in the sea creatures. You can talk to Him about your troubles and He will help you.

Jesus didn't shout down to you from the safety

of heaven. He didn't send someone else to give you a message. He didn't drop leaflets from the sky. He came!

He didn't arrive as a rich or famous man, nor flash His power around to make people notice Him, or use force. He came as a working man with little money or status. He came to live, laugh and cry just like you do. He came to die so you would have a way to escape the terrible storm- so you could live.

What He wants you to do is to recognize that you're in big trouble and flee to Him. Then He will take it from there.

### Discussion Questions

- In Honaunau Bay, I wanted to become a fish. How could that have helped the fish in trouble?
- When Jesus looked down into our world, He saw our troubles. He didn't think about becoming a fish. What did He do that was even more amazing?

The author diving the reef off Eleuthera Island.

# Chapter 4
# *Recovered Treasure*

I cruised along through the still water off Eleuthera Island, Bahamas. At 30 feet the sun probed down lighting up the reef so I could see the fantastic colors of the fish and sponges. As I approached a shallow cave, I turned over and slid, upside down, through the narrow opening. I pointed my dive light into the darkness, flashing it along the sides and ceiling of the cave. Not one fish swam about in the still water and no sponges clung to its sides. Suddenly I spotted a cone shell attached to an outcropping of rock. It looked small and colorless

"Just an old worn-out shell," I mumbled into my mouthpiece.

"Think again," a voice cautioned. "Remember that you can't see bright colors inside this dark cave, so the shell looks grey and old."

I plucked the drab shell from the rock, turning it over and over in my hand. It didn't look like anything special, but I reached into my net collecting bag and grabbed a small plastic bag. I opened it and placed the cone inside. The schools of beautiful fish soon made me forget about the tiny shell.

Ten minutes later, I checked my dive computer. A red light flashed at me, reminding me to surface soon. I kicked my fins and headed off toward the boat. Marilee, my dive partner, joined me at the dive ladder.

"What did you find under that ledge?" Marilee asked as I popped through the surface and climbed up the ladder into the boat.

We removed our tanks and weight belts, placing our masks, knives and computers into our dive bags.

"I found this little cone," I said, dumping the cone from the plastic bag into the palm of my hand. "I almost left it behind because it doesn't look like much."

"Do you know what you have?" she shouted, snatching the cone from my hand and holding it up for everyone to see. "You have a *Conus attenuatus* shell."

"I do?" I said, staring at the cone that now looked golden in the sunlight.

"This is a rare shell. You found it while slithering upside down in that cave. I saw your tank get caught in the sand and watched you wiggle free." She laughed and handed the shell back to me. "Take good care of that shell. You may never find another one."

"I will," I said as I dropped it into a clean plastic bag. "I will."

At home I gave all my gear a good rinsing and laid each piece out to dry. I unpacked and cleaned each shell carefully, laying them out on paper towels to dry.

After the shells dried, I rubbed them with a special solution of three parts baby oil and one part lighter fluid that I had previously mixed up and stored in a bottle.

I filled out a special slip of paper for each shell, writing the name of the shell, the location where I discovered it, the type of habitat where it lived, and any particularly interesting information I didn't want to forget. Then I gave each one a number and wrote their names and numbers in a special book. When I finished, I tossed the old plastic bags into a larger bag to be used again.

Several days later, when the last shell had been placed in the display cabinet where I kept my collection, I realized that the golden cone was not there. I searched everywhere and wondered how I could have been so careless with such treasure. I prayed and searched, prayed and searched, but did not find the cone. I thought about the lost cone several times during the next eight months, feeling sad that it was gone.

"Let's do some shelling on the mud flats," I said to Martha and my daughter, Sally, one morning. We packed up our beach clothes, snorkeling gear, and a lunch. I grabbed the large plastic bag where I stashed smaller used bags, and we headed for the car.

Sixteen hours later we arrived at Sanibel Island, and parked our car at a small marina that clung to the very end of the island. "We need a large canoe," I said to the dock master. He handed me some papers to fill out, and while I scratched in my name and phone number, he carried the canoe to the water's edge.

As soon as I paid the rental fee, we flung our gear into the canoe and began to paddle our way toward a channel of water that opened, on the left, into the sea. On the right sat the shallow bay where many seashells lived. We entered the channel and a strong current grasped us, drawing us straight ahead toward a boat dock. Very soon we neared the spot where we needed to turn right, away from the open sea, to go out to the bay. "Wow, look at that fog," I said, pointing to the bay. "I've never seen it so dense."

"The sun will burn it off soon enough," Martha commented, dipping her paddle into the water.

I plunged my paddle deep into the water and turned it, forcing the canoe to the right. We could see acres of open mud flats stretched ahead where the tide drained off the water and sent it out to sea. "The sea has pulled back," I explained, "and left the land all soggy and slick beneath the mist.

"This is a strong current," I said, suddenly noticing how fast we moved forward. "We're going to have a hard time turning right because it taking us straight toward that pier in front of us. We'll have to turn quickly or be slammed into the pilings."

I managed to turn the canoe toward the flats, but, in spite of our efforts, the current caught us and carried us sideways toward the pier. Martha and Sally thrust their paddles into the water and dug deep. We held our breath. "Paddle!" I commanded.

It was too late. The current grabbed us, pushing us closer and closer to the pier.

"We're going to hit those dock pillars," I screamed. "Grab your life cushion."

Crash! The canoe smashed broadside into the pilings, shooting us into the murky water like three cannon balls. I landed with a splash and heard two splashes as Martha and Sally hit the water. We disappeared beneath the surface. My ankle caught between the overturned canoe and the pier piling and I stifled an urge to scream. I managed to keep my mouth shut until my foot popped free and allowed me to surface.

I searched the water for my companions. Soon Sally popped up. Her wet face held a smile and her eyes shone with excitement. She swam over to the canoe that was filling with water. I turned in a circle scanning the water for Martha. She burst through the surface, eyes bugging out and mouth wide open.

"Grab the pilings and the canoe," I yelled, as the current snatched at us, threatening to swirl us away into the fog. I reached out and took hold of the sinking canoe and held onto one of the dock posts until both Martha and Sally had a firm grip, then let go.

The canoe filled with water. Our collecting gear rose up from the bottom of the canoe, piece by piece, and floated away into the fog. A paddle and seat cushion swirled past, followed by our lunch bag, extra clothing, and my camera.

"Hang on," I screamed. "I'm going to get some of our stuff before it disappears." I lunged into the current grabbing as much as I could before making a fierce struggle toward the rocky bank at the end of the pier. I threw the soggy things onto the rocks, snatched a rope that hung off the pier and started toward Martha and Sally.

"The end of the canoe is caught in the current," Martha yelled. "It's pulling away from the pier and we can't hold it."

"I'm coming," I said, sloshing through the water. Before I could grab it, the current ripped the canoe from their hands. They clung to the pilings and watched the partly submerged canoe float away.

I lunged after the canoe. "I've got it," I shouted,

grabbing the boat and dragging it onto the shore on the other end of the dock.

"Hey what about us?" Martha shouted.

I turned and swam toward them and threw one end of the rope to Sally and Martha. They grabbed it and paddled toward me. We sat on the rocks at the end of the pier and caught our breath. After resting a few minutes, we bailed out the flooded canoe, replaced our possessions, and climbed in.

"Let's paddle to the opposite shore," I suggested.

When we bumped into the bank, we climbed out onto the mud and looked at the soggy gear that lay in a heap in the middle of the canoe.

My camera was ruined. I felt so bad I had to turn away so Martha and Sally couldn't see my tears. That camera had traveled with me halfway around the world capturing pictures of all kinds of adventures. Now it would never take another picture. I knew it would be a long time before I could buy another. *When I do buy another camera, it will be a water camera,* I thought

I arranged the small amount of gear that I had rescued, making room for us to sit. Suddenly I noticed a plastic bag sitting on the mud. "Why did I bother to rescue that?" I cried, picking up the worthless bag. Sally and Martha just shook their heads.

When I threw the bag into the canoe, I saw a small flash of gold. I snatched up the bag, tore it open, pulled out a small cone shell, and held it up for the girls to see.

"That can't be the gold cone you found in the Bahamas," Martha said, staring down at the small shell.

"You must have stowed it away with your used

plastic bags by accident," Sally shouted.

"You grabbed it just before you headed for the car," Martha added.

We stared at the shell that I had found deep in the reef. It traveled all the way from the Bahamas to Maryland, sat hidden in a stack of used bags, then got dumped into the bay in Florida.

"It's a miracle," Sally said.

"You saved it from a fate in the bottom of this muddy bay," Martha said, smiling at me. "It would have been lost forever."

"Only God knew where the lost shell was. He prompted me to grab the plastic bag," I sighed, clasping the shell tight in my hand as if to keep it from getting lost again.

I put *Conus attenuatus* in a safe place deep in my backpack. "Thank you, God, for the shell that has helped me understand your business of search and rescue," I prayed, as we climbed into the canoe and paddled away.

Do you ever feel lost? I want you to know there is Someone out there who knows all about you. He follows you with His eye. And, He reminds you, in Acts 2:21, "Whoever calls on the Lord for help will be saved." Even if He has rescued you before, and you got lost again, He will rescue you once more. You will be twice saved and twice rescued and twice as valuable, just like my precious *Conus attenuatus* shell.

## Discussion Questions

- Why did I say in that story that the cone shell was twice saved?
- What do we mean when we say that Jesus rescued us?
- How do we know we are valuable treasure?

# Part 3

## I Need a Hero

*Choosing Jesus*

# Chapter 5
# The Crab That Can't Swim

Sargassum Weed, the chapter heading in my ocean book shouted. I wondered what kind of weed could live in the open sea. I rearranged myself on top of the flat rock that sat beside the green Pacific waters. Great breakers pounded the sand not far away. *This sea is so different from the one described in my book,* I thought.

By the end of the chapter, I had read enough to imagine what that weed must look like and could almost see the tiny creatures that lived there.

I shut my book and stared out at the ocean. Sunlight skipped across the surface of the water that stretched before me like a blanket whipped by the wind. I tried to imagine that I actually gazed far out over the great Atlantic Ocean to where the Sargasso Sea lay cluttered with the giant clumps of Sargassum. *The thick masses of yellow-green weed must get all tangled together,* I thought. That rubbery stuff sloshes back and forth in the lazy currents.

I opened my book again and read on. I discovered that the Sargasso Sea is a listless body of water covering more than 50,000 square miles. Currents of water, like rivers, run in a circle around the Sargasso Sea. They enclose the blanket of Sargassum Weed, keeping it together just as if surrounded by a wall.

Scientists, I learned, believe that pieces of the Sargassum break off from places in the warm, tropical waters further south and drift to the Atlantic where they snag against the tangled strands of weed already gathered there. The layer of weed keeps growing until it forms a whole mat of living islands.

The Sargassum does not need to be anchored to the bottom like the sea fans that clasp the corals in the Bahamas or like the Giant Kelp that grows along the California coast. It simply lays tangled up on the surface. Tiny, hard, air-filled balloons grow along the long stems. These keep the Sargassum floating on top of the lazy sea. Suddenly I wished I could slosh among the fronds in that strange sea.

I imagined taking a sleek sailboat far across the Atlantic. I could almost feel myself leaping from the pier into the boat. I'd stow my gear away and head for the deck to wave good-bye to friends.

Then, as the shoreline disappeared, I'd stand facing seaward. I'd taste the sea spray flung up by the wind and feel the ship climbing up over the swells and sliding down again, her sails catching the breeze and billowing out. Days later I'd arrive at the Sargasso Sea.

"It would be so much fun to discover the tiny creatures that live among the weed strands," I said to a sea gull that sat on a rock nearby, keeping me company me as I imagined my journey.

I scanned the pages of my book titled Sargassum Creatures. It amazed me that so many creatures could live far out in the ocean in a world consisting only of seaweeds and water.

*If I could just get out there,* I thought. *I'd lower myself over the side of the boat and move silently toward the loosely woven mat of weeds. I wouldn't frighten the tiny creatures, but just hang in the water with my head above the surface, looking out over the top of the weeds. The view would be a good one. Then I'd sink down a bit, breathing through my snorkel. I could spot the seaweed creatures easily.*

"I'd see all the crabs and sea shells that are described in this book," I said to the gull. He just sat there looking at me.

I imagined that my eyes would focus on the patch of weeds, staring at the olive-green strands. Sooner or later those tiny creatures would think I was part of the weeds and begin to move about. Then I'd get a good look at them. Perhaps I'd catch a glimpse of the tiny Sargassum Shrimp climbing on spindly legs over the Jell-O-like leaves.

If I stared long enough, a tiny Histro Fish, whose scales match the color of the weeds, would swish past. He'd hide among the vines, safe from predator fish looking for a good meal.

"It would be hard not to laugh at a tiny mollusk creature scrambling along the rough surface of the weed patch with its shell bobbing along behind," I said to a plump sea gull who sat watching me. "But laughing would let water into my snorkel. So, I wouldn't laugh. I'd just think about laughing."

I stopped gazing out over the sea and scanned a few more pages in my book. "What a strange crab," I shouted to the gull. He flew off in alarm. I stared at the picture of a tiny olive-brown crab that perfectly matched the Sargassum Weed. "This Crab Can't Swim," I said, reading the caption beneath the picture again.

"What!" I cried. "There's a crab living in the middle of the ocean that can't swim? That's crazy. What if it slips? One careless step could send it sinking into the black abyss below." The gull circled, squawking at me.

I paid no attention to the gull. I had to understand how such a crab could live on water without the ability to swim, so I kept reading. I learned that the Sargassum Crab spends its entire life adrift on the Sargassum Weed, clamoring over the thick surface. It must eat, sleep, and raise young crabs, right on top of the mass of vines where it is born.

I could just imagine the tiny green crab scampering along on the tangled vines. Perhaps it wanted to dash over to have a good claw to claw talk with a neighbor. I imagined it would stop at a small open place in the patch where only a few thin tangled weeds stretched across to its neighbor's patch of weed. I gasped, realizing that the crab might choose to balance itself on those tiny claws and cross the dark water on the thin layer of weed. The shortcut would look tempting.

Then I learned something that made me leap up and swirl around in joy. True, the Sargassum Crab can't swim, but it doesn't matter. The crab isn't worried even though the its home is surrounded by miles of cold water. The Creator gave the crab instinct. Instinct is like a set of instructions printed on the crab's brain. It tells it not to take the short cut. Instinct warns it to go the long way around because it's safer.

"What a wonderful Creator," I called out over the sea. "He invented instinct."

Then I thought of all the tiny crabs that obeyed the voice of instinct, telling them to stay with the thick tangles of weed and avoid the dangerous open places. Those smart crabs listen to the voice of instinct. They don't worry. They obey.

I closed my book and stuffed it into my backpack. The sea gull flew over, legs dangling, and landed on the rock. "It's all right," I whispered. "Everything is all right."

As I made my way down to the sand and toward home, I thanked God for inventing instinct so crabs could make their journey through the Sargassum Weeds safely.

You live in a world just as full of danger as the Sargassum Crab. You're expected to be good, make great decisions, use your time wisely, get good grades, and obey. Maybe you've discovered that doing all this isn't so easy. Maybe you've taken the short cut across dangerous waters and are sinking into cold, dark troubles right now.

Don't worry. God is your Hero. He knows your problems. He understands that you're being tempted to take some dangerous short cuts through life. He sent His Son, Jesus, to make sure you would stay safe and find your way to heaven. He also gave you a conscience that works even better than instinct. It helps you consider God's instructions in the Bible before you make decisions. It acts like an alarm that goes off when you are in danger of making a wrong choice.

The Bible says, in John 14:6, "I am the way you get to the Father. I'm the truth about what He's like.

# The Crab That Can't Swim

No one can come to the Father on his own. He has to come through me..."

So go ahead. Scamper through life like the Sargassum Crab. Don't worry. Just listen to God's voice and obey His instructions. Don't try tempting shortcuts through dangerous territory. If you do make a foolish choice and fall into sin, there's good news. You have a Hero, Jesus, who cares about a tiny crab that can't swim, and who cares about you. He will hear your cry for help and rescue you. He will forgive you and send you on your way again, a wiser and happier person.

## Discussion Questions

- Jesus gave the animals He created something called instinct. This helps them know what to do in nature. When Jesus created us, what did He give us that is even better than instinct? How does this gift help us make good choices?
- Why is Jesus the only one who can save us from our sins?

Barnacles and Blue Muscles cling to the rocks.

## Chapter 6
# The Storm Tossed Barnacle

The wind raged all night, blowing the sea up into great mounds of water and digging out deep valleys. It slashed into the black clouds, dashing them to pieces and flinging them across the dark sky. Suddenly, the sun peeked through a small space between the frowning clouds. At that moment, a baby barnacle was born.

He didn't know that he would someday look like his mother who sat on the end of a round stalk, like a gray butterfly, clinging to the side of a sunken ship. He had no idea that he belonged to the family of barnacles called *Lepas Antihera*. He just wiggled and sloshed about in the restless sea.

Then a current of water, like a flowing river, tore him loose and swirled him away. He rode up over the top of the waves and fell into the canyons of water. Up and down, he traveled over the face of the ragged sea. He swirled about with thousands of other little creatures that had been tossed into the water at their birth.

Inside the barnacle's tiny brain, a message played over and over. "Choose a strong, safe place to live. Flip over on your head and glue yourself down."

Soon the old sunken ship, where his mother lived, lay far away at the bottom of the sea. He couldn't glue to that.

The barnacle spotted a tropical fish decorated with blue and gold but it swished about too much. He didn't want to be flung about in the great sea. A strand of floating seaweed passed by, but it looked slimy and thin. *That won't make a good home,* Lepas thought.

A breeze moved Lepas, the helpless larvae, over the face of the sea. He continued to float right along with the other tiny life forms that searched for safe hiding places. Together they made up a soupy mixture of miniature plants and animals.

Again, the voice God put inside Lepas told it to find a safe place to attach. "You'll be sipped up by a hungry fish," it warned.

Lepas grew. He swam deeper and deeper into the sea. Suddenly he spotted a hard object in the sand and swam straight for it. It wasn't the bottom of a great ship, a rocky cliff nor even an anchored buoy.

Because of the long, wild ride on the angry sea, Lepas just wanted to settle down and get about the business of building a home. *Soon*, he must have thought, I'll be out of this mass of floating creatures and glued down to something hard and safe. That will be a relief.

Finally, Lepas reached the object. *This looks great*, he thought. It's a hard rock. So, without looking the object over with a careful eye, Lepas flipped over onto his head and squeezed out a blob of glue. He pressed himself against the hard object. When the glue touched the water, it hardened and held fast. Lepas did not know that he had chosen a coconut for a home.

# The Storm Tossed Barnacle

Soon the wind sighed and fell asleep letting the sea fall flat into a great quiet pool. Lepas felt safe clinging to the top of the coconut in the calm ocean. The tiny barnacle grew very fast. He worked on building a purplish-brown stalk until it stuck about three inches from the end of the coconut. Next, Lepas created a house of five white plates that fit together at the top. Now he looked like a plump butterfly perched on a flower stem.

When Lepas stuck feeding appendages through the opening in the top of the plates, they looked like tiny feather dusters. He swished them about in the water collecting tiny bits of food as the currents of water moved past.

One day the wind awoke him. It poked fingers into the water and stirred up the sand surrounding Lepas' house. Suddenly it lifted the coconut out of the sand. The coconut shot to the surface of the water. It spun about, tumbling up the front side of a wave. Lepas rode right along with it. He was glued tight.

A gust of wind grabbed the coconut and tossed it into the air where it twirled around and around until a wave reached up and snatched it. So, the wind and the water played catch with the coconut and the barnacle that clung to it. Finally, they carried Lepas and his coconut toward the shore.

A great wave flung the coconut and Lepas against the beach where breakers beat them into the sand. Lepas might have been buried and disappeared forever, but another wave lifted his coconut home up and flung it against a rock wall that jutted from the beach. The soggy old coconut cracked wide open and sent Lepas flying. He landed with a plunk high on the shore still attached to part of his house. The water trickled off the shaken barnacle and ran back to the sea, leaving him behind.

When I walked past the wall of rocks, I saw a tiny brown speck in the sand. I reached down and picked it up. I saw Lepas still clinging to the piece of coconut shell. His appendages lay limp and full of sand. Lepas was dead.

"You didn't choose a very good place to attach," I whispered to Lepas, running my fingers along his smooth house. "That storm really gave you a terrible time. I wish I could help you, but I can't," I whispered. I tossed the barnacle into the water and walked on down the beach. Lepas was beyond help.

Like Lepas, you start life drifting about searching for a place to attach. You have to choose, and just like Lepas, you have many options or possibilities. Some people choose money and the power it brings. Others choose the promised security of work. Some depend on their great talents or upon other people. They glue to those things. When the storms of life come, they find themselves in trouble like Lepas did.

The good news is that there is someone who can help. You can choose God, the Rock. You can attach to Him with the glue of love.

When the waves of trouble crash about you, you can count on Him to be a safe Friend. He's your true Hero, the one who loves you and died to give you the power to choose. Together you can ride out any storm that comes along. He will never stop being your best Friend.

If you have already glued yourself down to something that's turned out to be as unsafe as the place Lepas chose, don't worry. Lepas only had one chance to choose. Once he glued himself down, he was stuck. But God forgives. He helps you make better choices. He can even pry you from whatever you've glued yourself to, and attach you to Himself. No storm can separate you from Him. No wind of trouble can blow you off course. Jesus will carry you right into heaven's safe harbor.

Psalm 91:2 says that king David made a choice. He chose Jesus. "I will say of the Lord, 'He is my refuge and fortress, my God, the One I can trust.'" Make the right choice like David did. Attach yourself to God.

### Discussion Questions

- What did the barnacle attach itself to? Why didn't this work out so well?
- What does it mean when we say, "don't attach to the wrong thing? Why does Jesus call Himself the "Rock"?

# Part 4

## I'm Sorry!

*Forgiveness*

A Sunrise Tellin is cast ashore.

## Chapter 7

# *Captured by Currents*

I scanned the horizon for the first sign of the tiny speck of land called Wood Key. An hour ago, my friends and I had dumped our snorkeling gear and lunch into the boat, Amazing Grace. We tucked our gear into safe wooden storage boxes and found seats at the stern of the boat. Sid, our Bahamian captain, revved up the motor and we left Eleuthera Island far behind.

The azure waters stretched out as far as the horizon. No sign of land cluttered the view.

"We won't see the key for an hour," Sid called over the sound of the motors.

I dreamed of my first sight of Wood Key and its lone palm tree. I imagined the white sand and untouched beach. I couldn't wait to search for shells on the white sandbar that surrounded Wood Key. I didn't plan to walk the shoreline. I wanted to snorkel along the edges of the island.

I knew that few people made the journey to this small island, and the shallow band of water surrounding it held many treasures. A deep sea spanned out, for what seemed like forever, just beyond the small plot of land.

"There it is," I shouted. "Look at all that shallow water that rings the island. There's the lone palm tree sticking out of the white sand." I laughed. *This is as good as it gets,* I thought.

Sid squinted into the sunlight as he edged the boat right up to the island. His six-foot frame towered above me where I sat on the side of the boat, my legs dangling overboard. I watched his muscles flex as he dropped the anchor. It felt good to have him along. He knew about currents and sea creatures we needed to avoid. He could help tote gear, too.

I jumped up and grabbed my snorkel gear and collecting bag. When I leaped off the back of the boat, my three friends followed me.

Sid picked up his mask and fins and joined us. "When the tide changes, I'll call you by giving you three blasts of the horn," he said. "That would be a good time to head for the boat."

I gripped my collecting bag and looked around. Marilee and Anita set off on foot, sloshing through the shallow water toward the sandbar that circled the island. I followed Sid who, like me, always chose to be in the water.

We started snorkeling close to shore. The water felt cool. I could see over 100 feet in any direction. I moved ten feet off shore and followed the curve of the beach. Shells lay strewn about on the white sand. Every few minutes Sid disappeared below and returned with a treasure. He dumped it into my yellow net collecting bag. Whenever I sighted a shell, I dove down and picked it up.

Over and over, I plunged down, grabbed a prize

and added it to the bag. The empty bi-valve shells looked like alabaster butterflies resting on the sand. Sometimes I managed to collect more than one before I kick my way to the surface, and fill my lungs with air. The warm sunshine melted the hours away.

From time-to-time Sid stood up and looked around. *He's probably just making sure we don't snorkel too far from the island,* I thought.

I looked at the shells in my bag. It held dozens of Sunrise Tellins. The pink rainbow markings and the shiny surface intrigued me. They looked so beautiful. I wondered what predator had eaten the snail creatures that made the shells.

*This is my favorite thing to do,* I thought. *I love gliding along, discovering a shell and diving down to grab it.* But, suddenly I realized that I felt very tired. I stood up in the shallow water and looked around, catching my breath, and resting my heavy collecting bag on the sandy bottom. Sid kept finding shells and dropping them into my bag. I didn't want to stop him from finding more treasure, but I couldn't swim another inch.

I shaded my eyes with a dripping hand and searched the island for my friends. "What?" I shouted, staring in disbelief. "I'm looking at the boat ahead of me." It bobbed in the gentle, undulating sea. *That boat should be behind me,* I thought, *I left it behind long ago.*

"You just snorkeled all the way around Wood Key," Anita yelled, hanging off the side of the boat.

I stared at her. "The whole island," I sighed, staggering toward the boat ladder.

At that moment, I saw a beautiful Sunrise Tellin a few feet away. It shimmered in the sunlight that pierced through the water. "Just a minute," I said, jamming my snorkel into my mouth.

"Wait!" Sid said, "You've got to be tired and the tide is changing. It swoops around this island and it moves fast. The sand bar is covered already and half the island is under water," he shouted.

"OK," I called back through my snorkel. I dove into the water, kicked my fins and headed toward a very big Sunrise Tellin. I sucked in a deep breath, blew it out gently as I dove down, grabbed the treasure and jetted to the surface. Then I saw another and another. *This is fantastic,* I thought to myself. I felt renewed energy. I cut through the water like a bullet, stopping to dive down after another rainbow shell and sticking it into my collecting bag.

"The tide is changing. It swoops around this island and it moves fast," a voice inside me whispered. All right, I moaned, thinking of all the shells I would have to leave behind when I headed back to the boat. I didn't feel a bit tired. In fact, I felt like keeping up the hunt forever.

*Wait a minute,* I thought, *I'm moving along awfully fast. Something is very strange.* I turned and headed back towards the boat, but I didn't move forward very fast.

I stood up. The azure water reached my chest. *It's still shallow,* I thought. *I am getting farther from the boat than I intended. I better get myself back to that boat. This current is getting stronger.* Just then I spotted another Sunrise Tellin less than ten feet away. It was a beauty. It looked bigger than any I'd seen so far. *I'll get one more. I want to have extra for sharing.*

"The tide is changing. It moves fast," a voice inside warned again. I promised myself I'd stop soon.

I gathered two more tellins. *Hey, it's getting*

*harder to dive down after these shells,* I thought. *The water must be deeper.*

I planted my feet onto the sandy bottom and stood up. "Wow!" I said. The water now reached my neck. A strong current grabbed at me, threatening to pull me off my feet.

*I've got to get back to the boat right now,* I thought, holding the heavy shell bag against my chest. I lay in the water again and kicked as hard as I could. In a few minutes I realized that I wasn't moving closer to the boat, so I kicked even harder. My legs ached so much I knew I would have to stop soon. *I'm moving backwards in this water in spite of all my kicking forward,* I thought, groaning. *But if I stop kicking, I'll slip away into deep water.*

Three minutes later, my leg muscles screamed and refused to continue. I let the shell bag dangle downward from my hand. When it touched the sand, it acted like an anchor slowing my backward movement. Only my head stuck out of the water. I knew that the current was taking me further and further from the boat.

Suddenly I got an idea. I lifted the shell bag from the bottom, scooted it about a foot ahead of me, then let it rest on the sand again. I picked it up again and dropped it onto the sand, kicking furiously the whole time. I felt the current surge against me like a rampaging river, but the dangling full shell bag acted like an anchor. When I lifted my head out of the water to check my location, I could see the sand bar shrinking just like my strength. I knew the water would soon cover the bar and deepen around the edges. *By then the current will be so strong it will sweep me away into the open sea,* I thought. *I'm in trouble.*

**59**

I spit out my snorkel and threw back my head. "Help!" I screamed.

I saw my friends lounging about the boat, talking and laughing. One by one they looked up.

"Help!" I screamed again. Sid raised his hand to shade his eyes. He scanned the sea.

"She's over there," he shouted, pointing at me.

Sid grabbed his gear and threw himself into the water. He pumped his giant fins and thrashed his arms, moving toward me with the help of the current.

I lifted my head from the water. "I can't kick anymore," I screamed.

"Just hang on," He called.

I looked down. The shell bag started dragging along the sand, and I felt myself slipping backwards.

Suddenly Sid reached out and grabbed me by one arm. My legs flew out from under me and threatened to float away. Even though Sid stood more than six feet tall, I could only see his head and neck above the water.

"Hold that bag against your chest," He shouted. "Kick like mad."

He slipped his fins off. He dug his feet into the sand, bending his strong body against the current and dragging me along behind. I kicked my fins as hard as I could even though my muscles screamed for me to stop. Time stood still as we thrust ourselves in the direction of the boat.

"Thanks for not asking me to leave my treasures," I whispered as Sid lifted me into the boat, handing me my shell bag.

"You're no match for a current like that," Sid said looking down at me.

"I see that," I said, still clutching my shells. "I'm going to listen to your warnings next time. You know more about this sea than I do."

He frowned at me, then turned and started up the engine. Soon we sped over the top of the sea toward the harbor.

I don't know how long it took to get back to land. I fell asleep in a heap in the back of the boat, still clutching my shells.

The sea taught me a lot that day. I learned that I'm no match for a swift moving current. I'm weak. I learned to listen to someone who knows more than I do, and not to hesitate to cry for help when I needed it.

Are you caught in the current of sin or some trouble, being swept away like I was at Wood Key? You've probably already discovered that you're no match against Satan's powerful temptations. His currents of sin can grab you and carry you away. When you give into his temptations, he tries to drown you in guilt. The moment you discover your danger, cry, "Help, I'm in big trouble." Jesus will hear you.

For years, David, the shepherd boy, spent every day trying to escape evil king Saul. He knew he was in big trouble. He realized his trouble was bigger than his strength to deal with it. He cried out to God for help. He wrote about his experience in Psalm 34:4, 6. "I prayed to the Lord and He answered me. He delivered me from my fears . . . The Lord heard me and saved me out of every trouble."

The amazing thing is this. You don't always realize your danger right away. You don't know you are drifting away from safety, or that something as powerful as an ocean current has you in its grasp. You might even think you're rather strong and have nothing to worry about when it's a negative power outside yourself that is actually moving you along.

Your attention might be wrapped up in something that takes your minds off a real situation until you come to the realization that you're in big trouble.

Just say, "I'm sorry. I was wrong. I was careless." God knows your trouble before you are even aware of it. He will forgive you. He is ready to snatch you out your trouble just like Sid caught hold of me and lifted me out of the current. He put me in the safe boat. God knows how to lift you to safety and put you in a safe place.

### Discussion Questions

- At Wood Key, I felt like I was strong and moving fast. What was happening?
- How does sin act like a strong current?
- When we are in trouble and cry out to Jesus, like David did, what will Jesus do?

The author's Triton Trumpet discovered in Majuro.

# Chapter 8
## *Triton's Treasure*

For months I searched for the Atlantic Triton Trumpet shell. I looked at the pictures of tritons so many times I could visualize its brown and white zigzag markings, and the wonderful shine that covered it inside and out. I knew to look for a large shell that could reach twelve to eighteen inches, and that lived six to thirty feet deep in shallow reefs in the Bahamas.

I snorkeled along the thin line of reef that fringed Miller's Beach watching for the pink, sharp tip that would stick out of a crevice and tell me that an adult shell might be hiding until nightfall when it could wander the reef. I plodded across sand bars that bordered shallow reefs far from shore, looked in and around scattered coral heads strewn over sea floor, and poked between clustered corals in the reef.

"The Triton Trumpet is one of your best creations," I whispered to God. "I just have to find a good specimen."

# Triton's Treasure

Then one morning Anita, Marilee and I jumped into our jeep and jogged over a rutted road to a distant Bahama beach. We spent the morning snorkeling until our skin looked like shriveled prunes. My mouth felt sore from holding tight to the snorkel, and my eyes were red from salt water creeping into my mask.

Finally, we traded in our snorkel and masks for a clear plastic, look box. These two-foot wide, round boxes with six-inch sides, allowed us to see the sand below as we walked along pushing them ahead of us. We could see the edge of the shallow reef that ran in a line not far from shore. I reached down, now and then, to pick up a treasure. I had almost forgotten about my search for the Triton Trumpet as I enjoyed the way the sun shone down making the azure water sparkle like a sea of diamonds.

Suddenly I saw a pink tip of shell sticking out of a crevice between two coral formations. Instantly I knew I had spotted a Triton Trumpet. *Is this a piece of shell or a good specimen?* I thought, holding my breath.

"Come look at this," I shouted to Anita who searched nearby.

"Do you think it's a triton?" she asked.

"That's what the tip end looks like," I said, trying not to get too excited.

"Pull it out," she screamed, dancing about in the water.

I took hold of that pink tip and drew it, inch by inch, from the crevice. Finally, I couldn't wait another moment to know the truth. I drew the whole shell out.

"She's got one!" Anita yelled. "A whole Triton Trumpet."

# Triton's Treasure

Marilee splashed her way over to us. We stared at the beautiful shell.

"What a treasure," Marilee said. "You'll probably never find another one."

"Now to find the Pacific Triton Trumpet," I said, "It's even bigger and lovelier than this Caribbean variety."

A year later, my friends and I flew to Majuro, an atoll located in the South Pacific Ocean. The island looks like a giant doughnut with a shark bite out of it.

We spent our mornings helping a group of young people build a concrete block building so the children on the island could have a school cafeteria. In the afternoons we headed for the beach, snorkeling along the shoreline and diving into the protected lagoon.

While we laid the blocks to make strong walls, I looked out over the island and the sea beyond and prayed, "God, I know the Pacific Triton Trumpet that lives here is the most beautiful Triton of all. I want to find one so I can show people what a fantastic Creator you are. Please help me find one."

I searched and I prayed, searched and prayed, waiting for the moment my eyes would discover the Pacific Triton Trumpet in its hiding place. I could almost feel the smooth, shiny surface and see the lines and bars that made up its fancy patterns. But I had to return home to America empty handed.

Little did I did know that at the same time, on the very same island I had just left, a small boy had prayed a similar prayer. He asked God to help him find a beautiful Triton Trumpet.

One morning just as the sun eased itself over the edge of the horizon and painted streaks of red and blue on the canvas of the sky, the boy and his father pushed a little wooden boat across the wet sand toward the splashing waves. They shoved the boat hard and watched it lift up onto the mounds of water, then they jumped in and rowed with all their might until they cleared the line of breakers.

Once out onto the smooth water of the lagoon they put bait on several lines and threw them out into the sea. The father watched the lines. When one became taught, he jerked the line and pulled in a fish.

The boy prepared to dive. He did not own fins and a mask. He wore a ragged pair of trunks and swim goggles.

"I'm going to find a Triton Trumpet, Father," He called as he leaped from the boat and sank down through the azure water. He darted about the scattered corals like a reef fish, looking into every crevice. He searched along the reef edges and across the white sand patches. The Caribbean sun awakened the day as the boy dove and returned to the surface, over and over again.

"I just have to find one," he said to his father as he rested, hanging his arms over the side of the boat and dangling in the water. The boat drifted about the lagoon as the hours passed. The tropical sun turned gold and sent hot fingers of light down upon the sea.

On one dive, the boy flushed a flounder from its hiding place in the sand. He followed a fat grouper around a huge brain coral, but he didn't see the treasured triton.

The sun eased itself down other side of the sky and prepared to rest upon the horizon again. Just before it touched down, the boy spotted two mounds on the sand not far from the boat. He dove, kicking hard. He grabbed the mounds. "Triton Trumpets, he shouted through pursed lips. "Two Trumpets." He tucked one shell under each arm and headed for the boat that floated just above him.

"Father!" he screamed as he burst through the surface. "Two Triton Trumpets. I found them just sitting on the sand."

His father reached down and took the shells from his hands and pulled him into the boat.

The boy's father stared at the shells. "They're really big ones," he said. "And they're empty."

"The biggest ones I ever seen," the boy said, taking one in his hands.

"May I keep them?" the boy questioned, pleading with his eyes.

"We've got room for them," His father said, "But they don't look like much. See how they're covered with grey silt that has hardened over the months. A fisherman probably caught them and took out the snail before tossing the shells overboard.

The boy frowned. He took the Triton Trumpet from His Father's hands.

"Father, I searched a long time for these shells. I know they look awful, but I want to take them home. There must be some way to make them pretty again."

"Son," The father said, resting his hand on the boy's shoulder. "Just throw them back into the sea. Tomorrow we will come out into the lagoon again and search for better specimens. I don't think there is any hope for these."

The boy shook his head. "I want to take them home, Father," he said

The boy's father smiled. "OK," he said, drawing in the fish lines.

The two sat in silence as they paddled toward the sandy shore. They toted the big shells and the fish to their cottage.

# Triton's Treasure

The boy cleaned the shells, but he couldn't remove the ugly grey that coated the outside of each shell. He placed them on a shelf in his room, turning shells so he could see the bit of color that peaked from the inside.

"I want to clean these up, Mother," he said. "I know there must be a way. Then they will be beautiful."

"Perhaps God will show you a way," His mother said. "Go wash up, we are having a very important visitor tonight. Elder Folkenberg, the General Conference President, is coming to talk with our people about God's work here on Majuro."

All through supper the boy thought about what gift he could give their guest.

"I don't have anything valuable," he sighed to himself not paying close attention to the conversation among the adults.

"My wife just loves shells," he heard Elder Folkenberg say.

The words grabbed the boy's attention. He jumped up and ran to his room.

He returned carrying the two Triton Trumpets.

"I want you to take these home to your wife," he said.

Elder Folkenberg stared at the shells. "They're so big," he said, ignoring the ugly outer covering. "Thank you."

Elder Folkenberg placed the big shells in his suitcases, protecting them with his clothing. He completed his travels and headed home to Maryland, USA. When He arrived home, he unpacked those shells and handed them to his wife, Anita. "Triton Trumpets," she said, "But they are so hopelessly crusted."

A few days later Anita called me and I headed

for her house to see the Triton Trumpets. *God has answered my prayer at last,* I thought.

"These look hopeless," Anita said, holding up the two huge shells as I came in the door. "But there must be some way to clean them."

"They sure are ugly," I agreed, staring at the shells. Disappointment grabbed me.

"It doesn't look like it has a bit of color left," Anita signed. "I usually find that all the color has eroded from shells that have rolled around on the bottom of the sea like these have. But, maybe you can find a way to clean yours, she said thrusting one of the tritons into my hands.

At home, I soaked the triton in 100% bleach overnight. The next morning, I rinsed it off. The hard crust that covered the shell didn't budge when I tried to scrape it off. I put the shell back into bleach again and left it overnight.

The next morning, I tried to scrape it with a sharp dental tool. Scrape, scrape, scratch, scrape. The sounds of scraping could be heard all over the house. Day after day I soaked and scraped. My fingers hurt. I got behind in my work. I didn't have time to cook or clean the house, but I didn't care. I had to know if that shell could be cleaned and if some of the beautiful pattern God created in the shell still existed beneath the crust.

One day I saw a small spot of color show through. Excitement jumped up and down inside me. I worked on the Triton Trumpet every day for the next three weeks.

Finally, the day came when I dipped the shell into soapy water and laid it on a towel to dry. I mixed one ounce of lighter fluid and three ounces of baby oil together then poured some of the solution into my hands. I rubbed that shell as carefully as a mother rubs a baby's body.

I stared at the miracle before me. The shell that the fishermen threw away as trash had been found by a small boy and changed into something of beauty. Wow!

"You are just like that shell," God whispered into my heart. "I can see the beauty that is inside of you."

And it's like you, too. Your enemy, Satan, felt certain that if he could get you to sin, he could make you crusted with more sins until you looked ugly. He thought that God would throw you away. But God didn't. He found you and helped you to understand how ugly sin is. He asks you to say, "I'm sorry." He leads you to choose a better life. God forgives you and sends the Holy Spirit to live in you. This miracle brings you so much joy that you shine just like the beautiful triton did when I rubbed it down with oil.

Remember that oil, in the Bible, is a symbol of the Holy Spirit. He comes into your life to make you shine. He teaches and guides you. He helps you know Jesus better.

If you should make a mistake, He cleanses you again, helping you grow more and more like Jesus, just like the Triton Trumpet starts with a pink tip and grows to be a giant beauty.

When Jesus comes again, He will make everything beautiful like He made it in the beginning. Every crippled leg will be straightened and every blind eye will see. Every bent form will stand tall and every dream will come true. All God's people will be brand new inside and outside like the Triton Trumpet.

# Triton's Treasure

## Discussion Questions

- Why do you think I wanted to find the Triton Trumpet so much?
- We are all Jesus' treasures. What will happen to the sick and crippled when Jesus comes?
- When I cleaned the Triton Trumpet, what did I rub it down with? What does oil represent in the Bible?

# Part 5

## Becoming a New Creature

*Receiving a New Heart*

Three cowrie shells discovered by the author.

## Chapter 9
# *Miracle Covering*

Over the years I have tried to talk my friends into going out at night to find shells, but when the warm sun sets behind the horizon, they have always decided to curl up in bed with a favorite book instead. I felt very excited when my friend Martha, and my daughter Sally, chose to go out into the night to look for cowrie shells.

That morning we had snorkeled along the edge of a wall made of piles of huge rocks. I turned over as many of the smaller rocks as I could. But most of the rocks were just too big. When the three of us began to shiver from the cold, I decided to head for shore.

At that moment, I spotted a large flat rock just off the main wall. It wouldn't budge when I tried to flip it over. Sally and Martha grabbed a finger-hold under a ledge of the rock and the three of us pulled it over toward us. When the water cleared of disturbed sediment, we saw a brown spotted shell. I grabbed it and we let the rock fall back into place.

# Miracle Covering

Later, when we were back in our room, we looked at the beautiful, shiny shell.

"It's a Deer Cowrie," I said, pointing at the shell's picture in my shell guide. "What a beauty."

Sally grabbed the book and read it to herself for a few minutes. "Did you know that these shells only come out at night to feed on the algae that live on the rocks?"

"I told you that night is the best time to find shells," I answered, taking the book from Sally. I stared at the pictures. "There are two kinds of cowrie shells that live beneath those rocks."

"Wow," Martha said, moving closer so she could see the pictures of the two cowrie shells.

"Let's go back out to the rock jetty tonight and see what we can find," I urged.

To my surprise, both girls excitedly said, "OK."

That night, just before the sun slipped behind the horizon, we gathered together our collecting bags and headed for the rock wall. "It will be nice, for a change, to shell without putting on snorkel gear," I said.

"That's true," Martha agreed. "Especially since that water looks dark and cold."

We made our way carefully over the rocks in the fading daylight, heading for the far end of the wall. When darkness settled in, we started searching for the cowrie treasures.

"I've got one," Sally cried out, holding a shiny shell over her head. Martha and I struggled over and looked at her shell. "There's another one," she shouted, pointing to a rock not far away.

"They sure are slimy," Martha said, when Sally handed her the shell.

Just then I saw a cowrie oozing up out of a crevice.

A thin, slimy looking skin partly covered the outside of the shell. As I reached for the shell, the creature spread the skin over its shell, almost making it disappear. When I picked up the cowrie, slime oozed out into my hand. *Why so much slime,* I thought. *I hate this stuff.* I tried to wash it off, but it stuck like glue.

We scrambled over the rocks until we had a good specimen of the two varieties of cowrie shells that lived in the area. Finally, tired and cold, we headed home.

"The best way to clean a cowrie is to freeze it for a few days. When we thaw it out, the animal will slip out of the opening," I explained. "I don't like this part of shelling, but I need shells to study and show to the kids in my week-of-prayer programs."

"We could have taken a lot of them," Martha said. "I saw a dozen oozing over the rocks."

"I know," I answered, "but by taking only a few, we are conserving for the future."

After showers and a hot supper, we flung ourselves onto the soft couches in our room and grabbed books.

"The covering on the cowrie is called a mantle," Sally read, not looking up from her book. "It helps to protect the shell."

"That slime you find so disgusting helps protect it from enemies," Martha added.

"I wonder how the mantle protects the shell," Sally said, continuing to read. "The mollusk creature inside the cowrie shell produces lots of slime. This book says that when a big crab takes a hold of the cowrie to crush it, the slime and the mantle both make the crab's claw slip off."

"Crabs can't get a good hold on the shell, so the cowrie just oozes away into the safety of a crevice,"

# Miracle Covering

I said.

"Did you know that there are pigment cells along the edge of the mantle?" Martha said, pointing to a picture of a Zigzag Cowrie. "These cells paint the color pattern of the shell. If the cells fire off in a staccato pattern, spots appear. If they fire off continuously, a stripe appears,"

"It says right here that the mantle repairs any scratches or breaks in the shell," I said, looking up from the shell guide I was carefully studying. "That mantle is fantastic. I want to learn more about this cowrie."

Year after year I became more and more fascinated with the sea and its creatures. I watched every video I could get my hands on, learning from other people's experiments and experiences.

One day I learned that, John Stoneman, a Canadian research scientist and underwater photographer, led his crew of SCUBA divers into a reef to try a special experiment. He carried a gallon-size glass jar full of water down to the coral heads below his boat. One diver captured a small fish, slid it into the jar and screwed the lid on tight. He placed the jar between two small coral formations and backed away.

The fish inside the jar could not swim about in the normal pattern of a healthy fish. It banged about, hitting the sides of the jar, not understanding why it couldn't escape since it could certainly see out and watch the other fish pass by.

Stoneman stationed a diver nearby who held fish fragments out to lure a large Nassau Grouper that the divers had seen earlier in the reef. The grouper took the bits of fish and circled in for another and another. All at once it spotted the fish in the jar, swimming crazily about. As if reading a clear signal from some unseen place, the grouper sped over to the jar and rammed it in an attempt to grab the fish it could see acting weird. Of course, the grouper couldn't understand that glass separated it from the victim, so it slammed the jar again and again. Yellowtail Snappers also rammed the jar. I can only imagine how scared that little fish felt with enemies coming at it from every direction.

Stoneman and his crew learned that predators attack fish and other prey that behave differently. Predators seem to know when a fish is sick or injured and zero in for the kill.

The interesting thing about this experiment is that when Stoneman opened the lid and tried to shake the little terrorized fish out, it stayed inside. Even when he reached his hand into the jar, the fish moved about trying to escape his hand and stay inside the jar.

Stoneman had to take the jar to another spot on the reef and dump the fish out near a crevice. The little fish darted out and into the crevice where it knew it could be safe.

What amazes me is that although the fish must have been shocked to realize that the predators could not hurt it inside the jar, even though the jar was invisible, the fish came to the conclusion that the jar kept it safe. That's no doubt why it wouldn't come out of the jar until it saw a familiar and safe crevice. Only then was the fish willing to trade the jar for the crevice as a place to hide.

This fish actually learned to trust the invisible glass. It tried its best to stay within the protection of the jar even though it had no idea how the whole thing worked.

You might find yourself in a similar situation.

# Miracle Covering

The predator, Satan, thinks he can grab you up and destroy your life. He appears stronger and more powerful. Like little fish, that knew the truth about the dangerous grouper, you know that when Satan appears you need a safe place to hide.

Choosing Jesus means you have an invisible shield that wraps around you and protects you from the prowling predator, Satan. As you begin to trust Jesus and his protective shield more and more, you will become more confident in your thinking.

When you choose Jesus, He gives you the ability to think differently. In Romans 12:2 the Apostle Paul says, "Don't pattern your life after this world, but let God transform you from the inside out and give you a new way of thinking..." This new way of thinking enables you to stay close to God and trust His protection, even though He is invisible.

You learn to believe His words, and trust Him just like the little fish trusted the invisible jar. You learn to stay with Him when predators circle or even ram you. Because of your new way of thinking, you will begin to act differently. You will begin to walk through life with a new vigor, joy, and a feeling of security. Satan can spot the new you. He knows that the invisible God surrounds you. He knows that you are protected by the Creator's invisible shield.

It is God's light that forms this invisible shield. When you walk with God, you walk in His Light, and are surrounded by a shield between you and Satan. This light also makes you a new creature. As you live in His Light, you become a creature who loves and obeys God. You will trust Him for everything you need.

But wait, there's more. When you choose Jesus, He also gives you a covering or mantle, much like the cowrie shell. The Bible calls this mantle the Robe of Righteousness. Like the cowrie's mantle, this invisible robe does beautiful things for you.

The Robe is actually Jesus' own white robe. When God looks at you, He sees his beautiful Son. He sees Jesus' righteousness covering and protecting you. The Robe of Righteousness emits no covering of slime, of course, but Satan can see it and knows that his temptations will slip right off you. He knows that when you wear Jesus' white robe, you are a new creature. He knows that you now think in a new and wonderful way.

The mantle is God's presence wrapped around you. It helps you heal from any wounds you experience in life. Just as the mantle paints the cowrie, God's presence in your life makes you beautiful. The mantle, or God's presence around you, makes this possible.

The mantle is also a guard against danger. It protects you from Satan's attacks. It helps you slip from his grasp, just as the cowrie slips from the claws of the crab. The cowrie knows that it is protected. It knows it can safely come out at night and feed. It has confidence in the mantle the Creator has wrapped around its shell.

Like the cowrie, you can have confidence in the special mantle God has provided to you through His own Son, Jesus Christ. Shell collectors treasure the cowrie for its beauty. You are God's beautiful treasure. He is seeking you in the night to add you to his own collection. When you are in God's collection, you can trust that he will care for you and protect you.

# Miracle Covering

## Discussion Questions

- What does the mantle covering on the beautiful cowrie shell do for it?
- What covering does Jesus give us? What does this covering do for each of us?
- When we choose Jesus, we become part of His collection. What do you think this means?

Author as student nurse.

# Chapter 10
# A New Heart

L et's say that you have just decided to choose Jesus for your Lord and Savior. You join a group of kids preparing for baptism. Soon you walk into the baptismal pool and your pastor plunges you beneath the water and pulls you out again. What happens next?

Now you belong to the family of God, so you try harder than ever to be good. You endeavor to obey your mother and father. You struggle to get along at school and not give your teacher a bad time. No matter how hard you try, you still find yourself failing to reach that far off goal people call 'goodness'. So, you decide to study your Bible more, sing songs at church, and even join a group doing missionary work on Sabbath afternoon. Still, you find yourself being drawn to old sinful habits. You ask yourself, "What's going on here?"

That's a good question. I can tell you exactly what's going on. You, like many others, are trying to be good with an old heart that loves sin. Stop! Something has to happen to you now. No one can get good things from an old sinful heart. Let me tell you about the time I figured this out and almost fainted while learning it.

I loved my studies as a student nurse. I learned so many new things every day that sometimes I felt my head would burst. I also learned to do things where my hands and brain had to cooperate in fantastic ways.

One morning my nursing instructor told me I would have to pass a test in surgical procedures before moving on with my training. She gave me a picture of a tray table set up for surgery. I could see dozens of instruments arranged in rows on the small table.

"There are certainly a lot of instruments," I groaned. "What kind of surgery will this be?"

"This tray is the set up for open heart surgery," my instructor said. "Memorize the name of each instrument until you can recognize them in your sleep. Get a friend to act as the doctor and let her call them out to you. You already know that you have to slap the handle into the waiting palm of the doctor's hand. The surgery is scheduled for next Monday morning. Don't worry, I'll be right there with you," she soothed. "Don't forget to visit the patient, Mr. Web, in room 134 before the surgery," she added.

I practiced before school and after school. I recited instrument names while waiting in cafeteria line and before going to bed. "I'm ready," I said to my friends.

Sunday morning, the day before the surgery, I ran to room 134 to meet Mr. Web. "Tomorrow you will be receiving a new heart," I said.

# A New Heart

"Yes, I know," he answered, fear flickering in his eyes.

"Don't worry," I encouraged looking at his frail body. His lips looked grey. I could see that his blood was not moving through his body like it should. I listened to his heart with my new stethoscope and it sounded irregular and weak. I talked with him about what to expect and prayed with him, asking God to bless the hands of the doctors who would do the surgery. I left the room, shaking my head. *This man's heart is so weak he can't even walk to the bathroom. I hope the new heart will be strong,* I thought.

On Monday I scrubbed right along with the surgeons. A nurse helped me with the sterile gown and gloves. I held my hands up as I entered the operating room. I knew that this kept germs from my arms from getting on my clean hands.

My instructor stood beside a table that looked exactly like the one in my picture. She motioned for me to join her. I glanced about the room noticing the heart-lung machine that would pump the blood in and out of the patient, taking the place of the heart during the operation.

Doctors stood around the patient and waited until the anesthetist said the patient was asleep. A tall doctor on my left said, "Scalpel!"

I grabbed the scalpel from the tray and slapped it, handle first, into the doctor's gloved hand. He shot me a smile and sliced the patient from neck to stomach. I almost keeled over when I saw the layer of skin and fat that covered the patient's body cut apart. I looked over at my instructor. She nodded encouragement.

The doctor shouted orders for one instrument after

another and I handed them to him as I had learned to do. But, when he cut the sternum, or breastbone, and used large silver claws to spread the chest open, human organs looked up at me. I could see the heart beating in the patient's chest. I froze.

"Sponges," the doctor commanded, but I didn't move. "I said, sponges," he demanded, again. I just stood with my mouth hanging open. I was looking into a human chest and looking at a real heart. Slabs of fat deposits covered the heart, and grey stuff lined the blood vessels. The blood flowed into the machine and received oxygen before it came back into the patient. The whole thing was more than I could grasp.

My instructor pushed me to one side and handed the doctor the instruments he needed. I stood staring as he cut and clamped vessels and hooked the patient up to the heart lung machine.

Suddenly he snipped one last blood vessel and lifted the old heart from Mr. Web's chest. He frowned. "That heart could never be repaired," he said, and dropped it into the trash.

I stared at the old heart and then at the empty spot in the patient's chest. I couldn't speak. *The patient is dead. He has no heart,* I thought. *His heart is in the trash.*

In an instant a nurse entered carrying a red and white plastic lunch basket. "Are you ready, Doctor?" she asked.

"We're ready," he said. The nurse reached into the basket and lifted out a human heart. She placed it into the doctor's hands. He smiled. "That's a healthy heart," he said, placing it into the opening in the man's chest. I stared, speechless, as the doctor sewed the patient's vessels to the new heart.

# A New Heart

"I'm ready for the paddles," he said after a long time. A nurse handed him the paddles and everyone stepped back. A jolt of electricity plunged into the new heart. It started beating. Everyone in the room cheered. Mr. Web's color changed from grey to normal flesh color. I could hear the regular beat, lub dub, lub dub, lub dub.

The next morning Mr. Web sat on the edge of his bed and spoke to me. I smiled. "It's the new heart," he said. "Tomorrow I will walk to the bathroom."

I flunked my surgical test. But my teacher gave me another chance. This time I was prepared to see miracles in the operating room. I kept my head about me. But, I never forgot the sight of that man without a heart. I always try to remember the miracle I saw that morning when the new heart began beating.

When people talk about your heart, they mean your mind. God teaches that your heart has the same problem as Mr. Web's heart. It can't be repaired. Sin has ruined it. You need a brand new one. Your 'old heart' does not love God and it doesn't want to change. God promises to give you a new heart. The new heart loves God. It wants to do what is right. That's the miracle that comes to you when you choose God and become a new creature.

## Discussion Questions

- Why did my patient need a new heart?
- The Bible calls our minds our heart. Why do we need a new heart?
- What does our new heart love to do?

# Part 6

## He's Changing Me

Building a Devotional Life

One of the many bridges connecting the Florida Keys.

## Chapter 11
# The Smart Sea Star

The Bahama Islands appeared beneath our plane. They looked like a handful of green emeralds scattered over the sea. Swirls of white sand surrounded each one, and beyond that lay azure water. I wanted to jump right out of the airplane and drop with a splash into paradise.

"I can't wait to dive into that reef," I said to Martha and Janice who sat beside me, pointing to the thin line of the reef beyond the edge of an island just below us. Waves crashed against the Atlantic side, and quiet water sloshed against the Caribbean edge.

"That's a beautiful sight," Martha said. "I wish I could leap out of the plane right now."

"I wish we could parachute over there," I said, pointing to a small spot of land below us that sat like a green gem in a blue sea. "It seems so close to shore. Just look at the cliffs along the shore. That means a great habitat for sea stars and other treasure."

# The Smart Sea Star

Our plane landed on Eleuthera, Island of Freedom, and we stepped out into the moist, warm air. A line formed at the customs counter. Finally, our turn came.

"Why do you have so much luggage?" a policeman questioned.

"We're going to dive and snorkel along every inch of your wonderful coast," I said.

"Have a great adventure," he said slapping colorful stamps on our luggage. We stowed our bags into a beat-up looking station wagon and headed south to Palmetto Point and our cottage.

Three hours later, at low tide, the sea pulled back from the shore, exposing a great shallow area. We headed for the tiny island that sat just a half-mile off shore. When we reached the island, we stopped and looked around.

A young Cushion Sea Star.

*I just love turning rocks over that sit in shallow water,* I thought to myself as I adjusted my snorkel and mask, stuck my fins onto my feet, and plunged in. *A treasure hides under every rock, just waiting to be discovered.*

We worked our way around the side of the island that faced the mainland, turning rocks and checking for treasure. Each of us placed the rocks back exactly as we had found them to protect the habitats that the small creatures needed to live safely.

I watched Martha adjust her snorkel, then follow a tiny, squiggly trail left in the sand by a mollusk creature. It moved just below the surface of the sand. The thin trail ended in a lump. Martha slid her gloved hand beneath the lump and lifted out a beautiful shiny olive shell. She smiled and slithered on.

Soon the water got rough. As we reached the side of the island toward the open sea, it started really jumping about. Tiny waves slapped against us and tried to shove us against the scattered corals and rocks that lay on the sand. I glanced at Janice. She probably wants to quit now that the sea is so rough, I thought. But she kept on turning rocks, ignoring the fact that the water tossed her about at times.

*One more rock,* I thought to myself, *then we'd better get out of here. This water is getting wild. I feel like a feather in a windstorm.* I lifted a rock and stared. There sat a sea star as blue as the sky. It fit on the end of my finger. I marveled at the creature's beautiful pattern, then placed the rock back in its place on the sand, slipping the tiny bit of blue beneath it. "Stay safe under there," I whispered to the star.

I stood up and looked about. Martha and Janice popped up. We slipped off our fins and headed for the shore, agreeing to end our exploration until the next day. The wind grabbed handfuls of water and flung them at us as we walked along. We laughed.

"I'll never forget that small flash of blue," I said to Martha when we dragged ourselves from the water and started the hike back to our car. We turned and gazed at the tiny piece of land.

# The Smart Sea Star

"God hid so many wonders out there," Janice mused. We stood for a moment, remembering crabs that twitched, darting fish, waving anemone tentacles, and swaying sea fans. For the next two weeks we dove the island's reefs and wandered the shore.

"I wonder why we haven't seen any Cushion Sea Stars?" Martha asked one morning as we sat drying off in the tropical sun.

"I don't know," I replied "I really want to see one before we have to go home. They're one of the largest sea stars in these island waters." We searched under rocks, waded along the shore, snorkeled over grass beds, and dove along the reef, but didn't see a single Cushion Sea Star.

Soon the time came for us to climb into the plane and return to Florida. I sighed. It seemed like I left more of myself in the Bahamas every time I visited. Since I hadn't seen that special Cushion Sea Star, I knew that returning was inevitable.

We boarded the plane. I watched the islands disappearing from view as we neared Florida's coast.

"Discovering a species, such as the Cushion Sea Star, is dependent upon knowing what habitat it chooses to live in," Janice said, looking up from an identification book she held on her lap.

I pried my eyes off the islands below and looked at Janice. "So where do they live?" I asked. "I checked every sandbar around. I know they live on the sand because they don't have any suction cups on their undersides to help them cling to rocks."

"They do live on sand," Janice said. "But they like fast-moving water that brings fresh supplies of food and oxygen. Cushion Sea Stars go for strong currents."

"They must have a computer chip in their brain that tells them where to live." Martha said. "Every creature has a special home where they can thrive."

I thought about the sea star until our plane passed over dark blue water and landed in Miami.

"Let's go to the Keys before we head home," I said. "We can find the Cushion Sea Star there. The water is warm. There is a ton of sand and the currents sweep between the little islands providing lots of ideal habitats for the Cushion star."

No one objected so we climbed into the car and headed south. We drove to Key Largo and then passed over bridge after bridge that connects the islands.

"This is perfect. The tide is low," I said. "See how it's pulling the water from the islands toward the open sea and the reef. It swirls between these islands at a very good clip." I slowed down so they could get a good look. "In and out, twice a day," I added.

"Her heart beats faster whenever she discovers that the tide is low, "Martha said, looking out at the azure water.

"Stop!" Martha and Janice shouted in unison. I brought the car to a screeching halt beside the road. Martha grabbed her binoculars and jumped out of the car. She looked over the guardrail at the shallow water below. Janice headed down the embankment toward the water.

"Look!" Martha shouted, peering through her binoculars. "Isn't that a Cushion Sea Star?"

I looked over the rail. There sat a large orange blob. "It's a sea star, all right," I shouted, scrambling down the rocky bank.

"There's a sea star out there," I called to Janice who already stood knee-deep in the azure water peering out toward the reef.

"It's off to your right," Martha called from her perch above. "Be careful," she added, watching Janice sink into the soft sand.

"Go out a little further," Martha shouted. "I'm sure it's a sea star," she said, waving her binoculars at us.

"Oh no," I sighed. "You're shelling from a bridge with binoculars. What next?" But I smiled at Martha's creative thinking and waded further from the shore. My feet sank into the soft sand and the current tugged at my legs. I could see the faint outline of a very large sea star.

"Just a little further," Martha encouraged.

"You can get it," Janice said. She planted her feet on a tangled mass of sea grass. I took one more step and stretched out toward the spot where Martha frantically pointed. The soft sand snatched my feet pulling them down until my knees almost disappeared. I could feel the tug of the current swirling past. Suddenly, I couldn't move.

"It's right in front of you," Martha shouted.

"I see it," I said, reaching down and grabbing the blob of color. "I've got it," I screamed. "But I'm stuck!"

Janice struggled over to me and tugged at me until I popped loose. We inched our way to the shore and fell onto the firm sand. Then we looked at our treasure.

"It's a beauty," we screamed, turning the sea star over and over in our hands. Martha climbed down the rocky bank and grabbed the star from my hands. "This is the first treasure I've ever found using binoculars," she sighed.

Later, after unpacking at the motel, we searched

through our identification guides for a picture of the Cushion Sea Star.

"We found it in the channel between the islands because it loves that swift water," Janice reminded me.

"That's a smart star. It stays away from the murky bay, from rough rocks, and from stagnant pools. Those tides passing by twice a day bring lots of food to the star," Martha added.

"Smart is right!" I said, looking at Martha, who discovered the star without even getting her feet wet. After I snuggled into bed that night, I thought about the Cushion Sea Star. *It really is smart*, I thought.

The smart star chooses the right place to live where it can thrive and grow. It doesn't rebel and go over to a shore and try to attach to the rocks. It doesn't have one suction cup, so attaching is impossible. It slithers over the sand in shallow water that moves in and out with the tides twice a day. So, it thrives.

When you realize that you're in big trouble, that's smart. God helps you discover that there really is someone who is out there. He helps you choose Him as your friend and Savior. When you say yes to God, that's smart.

Day after day, as you live your life, you make mistakes. Don't worry! Don't let Satan, beat you up with negative words. He might lie to you and tell you that you that God can't forgive you. He could suggest to you that you'll never be good enough to please God. This, too, is a lie.

When you move into a place or 'habitat' that isn't where God intended for you to be, say, "I'm sorry." Realize your mistakes and tell God that you are sorry. Tell Him that you want to be more like Him and stay where you can thrive. He will forgive you and help you to choose the best places to be.

God sends the Holy Spirit to teach you that the best place for you is close at His side. You stay close to God when you choose to read your Bible, study nature, and talk to Him. His love will flow over you just like the two tides that bring fresh food and oxygen to the smart Cushion Sea Star.

### Discussion Questions

- Where does the Cushion Star love to live? Why does it choose this place?
- There are places where we grow best. When we go to the wrong place or make wrong choices, what should we do right away?
- How many times will Jesus forgive us?

Clusters of nerite shells sit on the rocks

## Chapter 12
# Shells That Choose Life

I walked along the edges of a great marsh that sat behind a line of dunes separating the land from the sea. The ground looked dry and cracked beneath the hot sun. I thought marshes always held shallow water, but this place looked like it hadn't caught a sprinkle of water for a long time. The earth had become so dry that it cracked into squares. The edges of the squares curled up. When I walked on them, they broke into pieces. I didn't see a bird or a lizard. Even the sea grasses lay drooped over the hot earth.

*It's so quiet around here,* I thought. *Where has everything gone?*

I passed beyond the marsh and climbed over the sand dunes that formed mounds of fine, white sand just beyond the reach of the sea. Gulls watched me slide down the front side of the dunes onto the wet sands of the beach. I stood up and picked my way over an outcropping of large rocks that sat just above the reach of the waves. Clusters of small, round nerite shells sat on the rocks like freckles on a boy's nose.

"Take a look at those smart nerite shells," a quiet voice inside me suggested.

"They're just common little nerites," I said. "What can they teach me? I already know that there are over 200 species of nerite shells living on rocky shores around the world. Most of them are no larger than the end of my thumb. The smallest nerite is only .2 inches. These tiny shells are a bright emerald green and are called Emerald Nerites, of course. I've collected several different species and put them in my collection, but now I'm off to discover something wonderful."

For three hours I walked and searched and thought. No new ideas came to my mind. I didn't see anything exciting. I didn't find a thing to write about in my notebook or to take a picture of. Finally, I felt so disappointed that I sat down under a palm tree and stared at the sea.

"Why doesn't God show me a new sea creature or an amazing shell?" I asked the gulls that soared overhead. They squawked back at me.

Soon I noticed that the tide was moving up the beach, so I picked up my empty collecting bag and started off toward my car. *I can't believe I've been on the beach this long and haven't seen one interesting thing*, I thought.

I scrambled up over the sand dunes and down into the marsh. It still looked as parched and dry as a lizard's skin. It still sat silent beneath the hot sun. I stopped and stared, shaking my head.

Just as I turned to walk on, I noticed water moving in from an inlet far off to my right. It flowed in long narrow streams like fingers touching the dry earth. It oozed up and surrounded the stalks of drooping sea grass, lifting fallen blades until they stood up again. It encircled my feet. Like an explosion, the whole dry marsh sprang to life.

The water soaked into the ground tickling the noses of tiny crabs that buried themselves and hid during the long, hot day. They wiggled and shook off the dirt that covered them. The cool water brought bits of food from the sea. They captured the tidbits and stuffed it into their mouths.

Black Mussel shells, clamped shut against the heat and dry air, now opened up a crack to take in the cool, life-giving water.

Birds flew down and landed on the now wet earth. They flapped their wings and scurried about. They ran on long spindly legs, back and forth, splashing in the shallow water with their spider thin feet. They jabbed their bills into the soft, wet earth. Up and down the marsh they ran, pecking, jumping, and dancing with delight.

*The tide is returning. It's wet, cool and full of food,* I thought to myself. *All God's creatures know this and have come out to meet it.*

"That's just what I've been trying to show you," a quiet voice inside me said.

"The nerites on the rocks?" I shouted. "They're part of this miracle and I walked right past them." I turned and rushed across the marsh, and up over the dunes toward the sea. The flat rocks sat dry and empty. I searched for the nerites but not one clung to the rocky surfaces.

"Where are the nerites?" I cried to the gulls, looking down the face of the rocks. I looked closer. The wind had laid a thin dusting of sand on the rocks. Suddenly I spied miniature trails etched in the sandy covering.

"The nerites made these trails through the sand as they oozed across the rocks, "I shouted in excitement."

I followed the trails. Every trail ended near the bottom of the rocks, and at the end of each trail sat a tiny nerite. The shells did not move close to the thrashing incoming waves. They sat above them, yet close enough to catch the splashes of water that flew into the sky as each wave hit the rocks.

"They're soaking up the sea spray," I cried out to God. "You've taught them to go out to meet the returning tide that brings them life. The droplet of water they trap inside their shells will help them live another day because it's full of oxygen and food."

I suddenly realized that not one nerite said to itself, "I don't have time to leave my place on the rock today, just to go down and meet the water." Each one climbed down the face of the rocks. Not one nerite said, "I don't need any water today. I have enough. I'll go another day." Every nerite climbed down the face of the rocks. Not one nerite said, "Why does it have to be water? I'd like to try to drink something else for a change." No! The rocky cliff was empty because each shell left its place and made the long journey down to the sea.

I stared at the miracle of the returning tide. I watched wise nerites go out to meet the incoming tide and laughed as tiny crabs gobbled up the good food the sea brought. I heard mussel shells click open and drink in the cool water. This made me sing as I watched the birds dance and prance about for joy at the return of the sea," It's a wonderful miracle, I shouted to God, who, no doubt, looked down and agreed with me.

"What about you?" A quiet voice inside me asked.

## Shells That Choose Life

"Me?" I asked.

Then the wonderful lesson jumped into my head. Every morning and evening the tide pulls the sea beyond the rocks and the marsh. But the sea creatures don't worry. They've stored water inside themselves. They know the tide will return and they all go out to meet it with joy as it comes flowing in. They receive life from that water to live another day. The nerites are so smart that they don't wait for the water to come up the side of the rocks. It never will. They go out to meet it.

The birds watch for that trickle of water to return to the marsh, then they fly ahead of it and wait for it to fill the marsh and awaken tiny things hidden under the mud, and they fill up on life-giving food. Even the crabs come to life, throwing off the dirt and grabbing up the food that floats in.

You are one of God's creatures. You need Him. He is your Water of Life. If you want to grow and be full of life, you need to go out to meet Him every morning and evening. You need to drink in all the love and joy that He brings to you.

The nerites know long before the tide brings the sea close to their rocks that it's time to head down the cliff. They know that if they wait too long or think they can skip a tide, they will die. They always choose to head for the sea.

Like the tiny nerite shells, you can make the right choice. These little sea creatures rush out to meet the returning tide. Will you rush out to meet God? Will you let Him fill you with His joy and change you until you are just like Him?

I felt so excited about these new thoughts and ideas that I began to dance like the birds and prance like the crabs, and I opened up my heart just like the mussels. I ran down to the water like the wise nerites.

"God, You will be my High Tide? I said. "Every morning and evening I will come out to meet You and read Your words. I will be as wise as the tiny nerite shells. I will be thirsty like the mussels, and as hungry as the crabs. I will be full of joy like the water birds."

My heart fell down on its knees and thanked God for His sea creatures and what they taught me that day out on the marsh by the sea.

### Discussion Questions

- What did I mean when I said: "the nerite shells choose life"?
- How can we copy the nerite shells?
- What happens when we forget to go out to meet with Jesus, morning and evening, to spend time with Him?

# Part 7

## Now I'm His Partner

*Sharing Jesus With Others*

The author searching for abalone shells at Laguna Beach.

# Chapter 13
# *Lost Abalone*

I stood at the top of the ridge that formed a giant half-moon body of water called Monterey Bay. I knew that most of California's coast consisted of scallop shaped bays and open shores, bordered by piles of rocks that fall from the cliffs. Sparkling water lapped against the scattered rocks, sending spray high into the air. Houses with observation porches and decks nestled themselves among the bumpy hillsides just beyond.

I felt the urge to slosh among the tide pools formed by clusters of rocks. They held water long after the tide pulled the sea back. November winds raged through surface water twisting it into formations and throwing it my way. *That water is far too cold for me to wade into,* I thought. The gusts that blew the water about tore at my hair and scattered goosebumps across my skin.

Suddenly I got an idea. I raised my field glasses to my eyes and scanned the clear water just below me. I spotted a tiny abalone shell, caught among the rocks, and climbed down the cliff snatching it up just before a wave could catch me. *Hey, this is the way to shell on a wintery day!* I thought.

After a while I got tired and sat down to rest. Fat sea lions looked like old rugs slung over the rocky breakwater to dry. They kept up a continuous barking sound.

Out of the corner of my eye I noticed a sea otter gliding along on his back. He flipped his finned feet and floated into the harbor, coming closer to the place where I clung to the rocks. I could see that he held a huge abalone shell upside down on his stomach. He took a bite, washed his whiskers with two front paws and stuffed another bite into his mouth. Then he rolled over in the water, using the sea like a napkin to remove stray bits of abalone from his hairy chest. Every second brought him closer to my spot on the rocks.

I held my breath as he glided within ten feet of my perch. He paused, rolled over, and came up licking the now empty shell. I really got excited, but hardly dared to move lest he spot me and swim away.

I grabbed my shirt and held it down so it wouldn't whip in the wind. Soon he turned over again, letting the empty shell drop into the shallow water. Scanning the sandy bottom with my binoculars, I could see that abalone sat not more than ten feet from shore in very shallow water. It glistened like an under-water rainbow. I could see reds, greens, blue, and gold colors. The kid in me began to jump up and down.

I pulled off my sweatshirt, pushed up my shirtsleeves, and plunged in. Frigid water enveloped me. I gasped, but kept my eyes on the shell. The wind clutched at my wet clothes, but I kept moving toward my prize. "Help me reach it," I prayed. "I just have to get the abalone that the sea otter brought right to me. Please, please let me get it."

The water surged back and forth as I struggled to reach deeper water. It threatened to push me over, but I didn't move my eyes from that shiny abalone. Higher and higher the water crept until it reached my armpits. I wished I'd brought my mask and snorkel so I could just plunge under and grab the shell. *How would I ever have guessed I would need to duck under this freezing water,* I thought.

When the water reached my shoulders, I touched the shell with a sneakered foot. *I've got it,* I thought. But, when I realized I would have to go completely under the water in order to grab the shell, I hesitated. *I just can't dip my head under,* I thought. *There must be another way.*

"I'll scoot it toward the rocks," I shouted to no one. "When I get it in shallower water, I'll reach down and grab it."

I gave the abalone a gentle nudge, then another and another. A swell caught me and nearly knocked me over, but I kept moving the shell closer and closer to the rocky shore.

When I stopped in waist deep water, I tried to pick the abalone up, but as I bent over the water caught my face.

"Wow! That's cold," I shouted. I'll have to push it into even shallower water. *I just can't stand to get my face and hair wet,* I thought.

I gave that abalone another shove. Suddenly it disappeared from sight.

"Oh, no" I cried, staring into the water. "Where did it go?" I couldn't see the abalone even though I looked everywhere.

My shivering body begged me to give up and get out of that cold water. I knew I needed warm dry clothes, but hated to give up the search. I stood and memorized the exact spot where the abalone disappeared, but at last the cold forced me from the water. I shivered all the way to the car. People stared at me as I ran along the road, water dripping from my pink sweat suit. I didn't care. I wanted to find a way to recapture my prize, but I couldn't think of anything. I felt far too cold to think.

When I reached the car, I rummaged around in the trunk. I saw my inflatable view box. *That's it,* I thought. *I'll fill this with air and be able to see clearly into the water.* I felt excited as I ran back to the water's edge and waded in. I put the cone shaped view box into the water, holding onto the handles on each side. I scanned the water looking to the right and left. The view box allowed me to see all the way to the bottom, but I still couldn't find the abalone.

*No one up in heaven has answered my cries for help,* I thought. *I wonder why?* Soon the cold dug deep inside me and I started to shake. I decided to give up the search. Tears came spilling over my cheeks.

"Why didn't you help me find that abalone?" I questioned God. I know you sent that sea otter along, but why couldn't you help me get it to shore? Then I realized that maybe God had a lesson for me. I felt so disappointed that I didn't really want a lesson. I just wanted that great big abalone that shimmered like a rainbow in the sun. I longed to touch the very abalone that the wild sea otter had brought me.

Later, after I wiggled into dry clothes and drank hot herb tea, I discovered the lesson. It's a great lesson and I think it came at a good time. When I thought about my experience, I realized that gaining a treasure might cost some sacrifice on my part: dunking my head below the surface into freezing water. If I wanted the treasure I needed to go ahead and give my all. The abalone would be worth it. I just hadn't been willing to do that.

When you choose Jesus, you become His partner. One thing that Jesus loves to do is to help others learn about Him, so He needs the help of those who know Him. He needs your help.

If you see a new person entering your Sabbath School room, realize that Jesus may have nudged them into your classroom. You want them to discover Jesus, just like you did. You also want them to come back again. So, you need to put your whole heart into helping that person become comfortable, and feel important. They are like a treasure. You don't want them to get away. You do everything you can to be friendly and encourage them to return because they are treasure.

I really wanted that abalone, but I stopped short of investing my whole self in getting it. I didn't want to get my face wet. So, somewhere on a rocky harbor edge, lies an abalone shell that will never be seen again. Winter storms will bash it against the rocks and break it to pieces. It's lost. I feel sad whenever I think of it. I also think about how wonderful it might have been if I had it to share with others and look at from time to time enjoying the bright colors and the shine.

The abalone is only a shell, but people are real treasures. You have the ability to find them and share what you know with them. This is what it means to be partners with God.

## Discussion Questions

- What happened to the beautiful Abalone shell that the Sea Otter brought to me?
- What more could I have done to capture that treasure?
- Jesus wants all kids to come to know Him and choose Him. How can we be his partner when we meet new kids who come to our church, neighborhood, or school?

A pair of Queen Conchs.

## Chapter 14
# George

I'll be back by 12:00 so we can go shelling," I yelled at Thelma. George eased the dive boat from the shallow water and we headed out toward the reef.

"Don't worry," George called to Thelma. "We'll be back in time for you girls to go out on the sand bar at low tide."

"You just can't wait to use your new gear," Thelma shouted. "I can't see how you're going to use that new lift bag. I know that you can put almost 50 pounds of shells or rocks in it, and as soon as you puff a little air into the air compartment, the bag will come right up to the surface. There's nothing out there that heavy."

"What a wonderful piece of equipment," I said, imagining finding a shell that big and watching it lift off the sand inside the new lift bag. "I'd like to see how it works."

"I hope you get to see it," George said, grinning at me.

# George

*Whew,* I thought. *In the morning I dive with George, and then I have to keep up with Thelma as she moves along the sand bars like a sanderling all afternoon.*

I didn't have more time to think about the busy day ahead because George stopped the boat near the reef and threw over the anchor. We suited up and I jumped off the back of the boat. The cool water swallowed me. I sank to the sand below and waited for my dive buddy to join me on the bottom of the sea.

Just as soon as George reached the bottom, he gave me the OK signal and turned and headed off across the sandy lagoon toward the reef. George didn't stop to poke around looking for shells. He cruised along the reef, pumping his big fins. I followed, making my small pink fins go as fast as I could. He slithered through a narrow cave. I followed. He rose up over the top of the reef and down the other side. I followed, stopping only long enough to peer into a sponge.

Then I spotted some small rocks scattered along the edge of the reef. I wanted to turn every one of those rocks over to see who lived underneath them. I knew that tulip shells, brittle stars, and crabs chose rocks as hiding places. I was tired of cruising and trying to keep up with George.

Suddenly he stopped to stare at a grouper being cleaned by cleaner shrimp. I had my chance. I didn't stop. I just kept swimming straight ahead. Empty white sand spread out in every direction, but I headed for the rocks.

I turned over a flat rock the size of a dinner plate. A tiny blue sea star looked up at me. George caught up with me and stared at the little star. He looked surprised that such a beautiful treasure could be found beneath a rock. I signaled for him to turn over a rock over that sat nearby.

George lifted the rock and a brittle star, covered by tiny hairs, darted off. It squeezed beneath another rock. George lifted that rock and the brittle star dashed for cover under the rock I had just laid back into place. *I hope it gets along with the blue starfish,* I thought, laughing to myself. We lifted rock after rock, finding scallops and crabs, and holding them up for the other to see.

After awhile, we found ourselves in a great sandy field, called a sea lagoon. I knew no shells would dare to walk around out there in the open, and that God wrote a message in each shell's brain that told them to stay hidden during the day. It reminded them to hide under a rock, slither into a crack in the reef, and stay hidden. I knew that every sea creature obeyed the message in order to stay safe.

I signaled George that I wanted to return to the reef. I knew that I would be able to discover more treasures where rocks and corals clustered together. We just started to turn around and head back for the reef when we saw an amazing sight.

There on the white sand sat the biggest Florida Horse Conch I'd ever seen. I headed right toward it. Then I noticed that it was connected to a big pink Queen Conch. George and I hovered over the two big shells. We looked at each other and both shrugged our shoulders as if to say to each other, "I don't know what they are doing, but they are in danger out here in the open."

The shells twisted and turned in the sand, sending sand particles up into the water.

"They are fighting!" I wanted to tell George, but

couldn't talk without losing my air supply.

Both of them have forgotten the message God wrote inside their brain and they both came out from hiding places. They thought they were strong. They thought they could ignore the warning messages in their brains. They forgot all about the danger around them from enemies larger than themselves. We both stared at the foolish shells that held each other in a death grip, each trying to eat the other.

We realized that they would only destroy each other, or be killed by a passing enemy, so we decided to try to separate them and take them to the boat. George motioned for me to grab the great Horse Conch. He clutched the Queen Conch. We both pulled and pulled. Suddenly the two shells came apart. George and I both fell backwards onto the sand. It didn't feel very good because lying on a round metal air tank is not comfortable.

I struggled to turn over, kicking wildly with my fins, still grasping the Horse Conch. I looked at George. He held the pink Queen Conch in his hands. Neither creature seemed to be alive. Parts of both their bodies were missing. They had started to eat each other.

George gave the thumbs up sign to signal that we should go up to the boat. We both kicked our fins as hard as we could, but we hardly rose in the water. I finally gave up and settled onto the sand. George signaled me that he would take his shell up and return in a few moments. He rose up to the boat and climbed in.

Five minutes later, George leaped overboard and sank down beside me. He held the lift bag in one hand. I put the horse conch into my collecting bag, and George hung it on the large hook at one end of the lift bag. He released a blast of air from his air tank into the parachute-like sack at the top of the lift bag. The air lifted the shell right up to the surface. We followed and climbed into the boat.

George found a measuring tape in a small tool kit and laid it alongside the Horse conch. "This Horse conch measures twenty-two inches long," he said. "The longest Horse Conch on record is only one inch longer."

When I returned to the hotel room, I showed the huge shell to Thelma.

"I guess he got a chance to use his lift bag," she laughed. "How are you going to get the dead animal out of it?"

"I'll find a way," I said, staring at my prize.

We filled the largest pan we could find and cooked one end of the shell for thirty minutes. Then turned it around and cooked the other end. I thumped the shell on the sand to loosen it. The dead animal fell out. Its body was twirled around and around the inner post called the columella. It looked like a girl's ringlet curl.

"I'm naming the Horse Conch, George," I said, laughing.

George cooked the great Queen Conch. It was a beautiful specimen.

That night as I lay in bed, I thought about the way George and I worked together to rescue the shells. We dove as a good team. I also thought about the shells. *Both of these shells would still be down deep in the sea if they had just remembered the message written in their brains and stayed under cover. Instead, they started fighting each other and they both lost. They were not a team,* I thought.

We sometimes act like these two shells. We don't

pay any attention to the messages God has given us in His Bible. We fight, complain, gossip, or just get too busy to help each other. Then our enemy, Satan, can easily snatch us away, just like we did those two careless shells.

God knows about this problem. Look what He says in His Word.

"I will put my laws in their minds and write them on their hearts, and I will be their God, and they will be my people." Jeremiah 31:33

Do you have trouble remembering God's messages? Do you have trouble finding time to study His Word? You can ask God to write His words on your heart and mind. That's His promise. Then you won't be overtaken by an enemy like these shells were.

### Discussion Questions

- What were the two big shells doing out in the open instead of hiding like instinct told them to do?
- How is instinct, that guides animals, different from the power to choose that Jesus gave to humans?
- In order to help us learn to obey His laws, what did Jesus do?

# Part 8

## I'm Connected to Power

The Power of Prayer

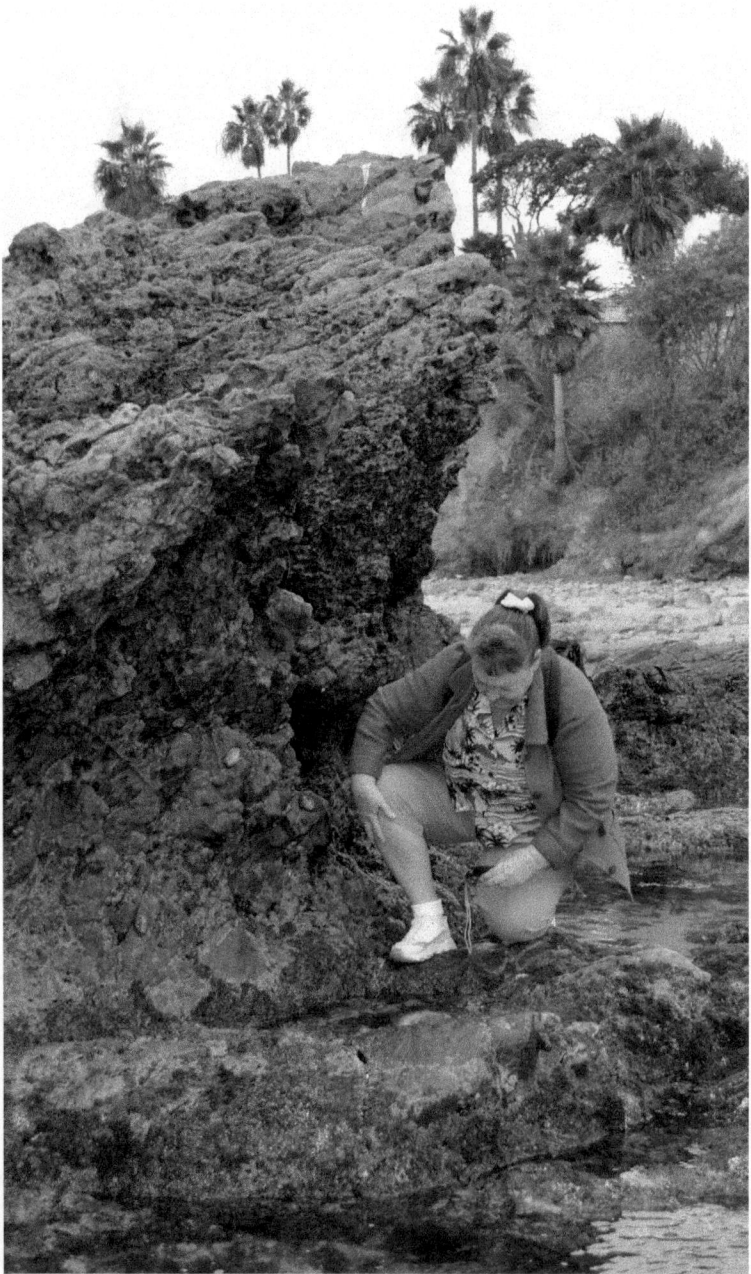

Author searching for limpet shells at Laguna Beach.

## Chapter 15
# The Sea Gull's Secret

Sharp gusts of wind flipped my hair about as I edged down the face of the cliff that jutted out into the sea. The red pack perched on my back lurched to one side as I stretched one leg to the right and fumbled for a new spot to jam my sneaker. My hands moved across the face of the cliff, searching for knobs of rock that might be hidden beneath the slimy seaweed. I grasped one and stopped to rest for a moment. A taste of salt hung in the misty air and sea gulls screamed at each other.

Inching toward a smooth place among the rocks, I turned and sat down. Suddenly a giant wave of green water rose up below me, trembled a moment, then tumbled toward the place where I clung to the rocks. It flung white foam into the air and small fingers of froth reached into the tidal pools nearby where speckled fish darted about. The wave set the silken tentacles of sea anemones waving in the clear water. As if by some silent command, the wave pulled back into the sea, leaving everything dripping with bubbles and tiny waterfalls.

I laughed into the wind. I smiled, thinking of my friend, Martha, who had said, "What's there to see at the ocean on a cold winter day when you can't go diving or swimming?"

She had given me such a puzzled look when I said, "I'm off to hunt limpets." Then she waved me away and returned to snuggle beside a warm fire in the cottage.

Searching along the cliff's face, I looked for the tiny shells that sat sprinkled about the rocks like freckles on a boy's face. Soon I found them near the low tide line. I saw hundreds of cone-shaped shells no larger than my fingernails. They clung to their home on the cliff just above the water.

I decided to take one of each species for closer study. When I reached out and touched one with my finger, it clamped itself against the rock with a sudden jerk.

I moved away before another wave tossed itself against the rocks. After the wave returned to the sea, I could see that all the limpets remained as unmoved as if they'd been touched by a feather instead of a boisterous wave.

"Wow!" I said to a circling gull. "They really stick, don't they?"

I poked around in my pack and found my dive knife. No matter how I tried, I could not slip the blade beneath the shell before it clamped down. When I forced the knife between the limpet's shell and the rock, I only managed to chip an ugly hole in it. No amount of twisting or pulling with my fingers would make a single shell let go. When I thumped the limpet with my knife handle, it clung tighter than ever.

"Nothing moves one of these wave-resistant midgets from the rock," I yelled at a cranky sea gull that soared past.

The gull squawked out some saucy complaint at me and landed nearby, watching my attempts to collect the limpets. All at once it grabbed a small stone its bill, rose into the wind and circled overhead. Two white wings hissed past. I heard a clunk and a plop.

At that instant, I saw a limpet bobbing helplessly in the tide pool below me. Before I could move, the sea gull dipped down and grabbed the limpet with his bill. Giving me a smug look, it flew off to sit on a huge rock far above me.

I struggled up the cliff toward him, waving my arms about. The gull let me get within ten feet of its perch before flying to another spot where I couldn't follow. I reached into the pool of water and lifted out a small, brown limpet shell. It contained tiny bits of gray flesh that the seagull left behind.

A Keyhole Limpet clings to a rock.

*This is amazing,* I thought. *All day giant waves smash against the limpets. They don't fall off.* I tugged and twisted them with my fingers. They just hung on. Even with the knife, I couldn't remove a shell without breaking it. Yet, when the sea gull chose one particular limpet, then dropped a rock on it, the limpet just fell off. That pesky bird knows something that I don't.

I returned to my pack and opened the shell guide, looking up the word, limpet. I learned that a limpet sticks to the rocky cliff by a big suction cup.

"That makes sense," I said, pointing at the gull, "If it held on with a muscle, eventually that muscle would get tired and limpet would just fall off. But how did you get it loose from the rock?" I asked the gull who still sat near me.

The sea gull only stared at me, so I read on. I discovered that limpets ooze over the rocks, grazing on algae, like tiny cows in a field. But they usually do this at night when darkness covers them with a black, protecting blanket. They squeeze out tiny chemical trails as they move along over the rocks. Limpets can follow these trails back to the special spot on the rocks that they call home. No other limpet will follow another limpet's trail. They make their own trail that leads to their home.

Leaping up, I shouted, "That's amazing!"

I continued to read and discovered that sometimes a limpet releases its suction cup enough to move along the rock in the middle of the day instead of waiting for the cover of darkness.

Somehow the sea gull knew this. He could see that most of the limpets held tight with the tiny suction cups God gave them. But the moment one limpet loosened its hold on the rock, the gull dropped the stone, knocking it off the rock and sending it tumbling into the tide-pool.

I looked at the limpets scattered about the face of the rocks and watched the circling gulls. All the limpets clung tightly to the cliff and the gulls soared away to look for other victims.

Satan, your enemy, knows a secret. He knows that you have the miracle of love that holds you to God, your Rock. He also knows that often guilt over your mistakes loosens your hold on Him. He also watches for you to become careless and forget to talk with God and read His messages in the Bible. That's when he swoops by and drops his rocks of discouragement on you. Then he circles in for the kill.

The great rocks along the shore to provide a safe place for the limpets to live. God gave them a perfect way to hang on. He imprinted a message into their brains that tells them to clasp the rock and only loosen their hold under the cover of night.

These small creatures teach you that God is your strong Rock and you can hold tight to Him. If you ever find yourself slipping away from God, admit your mistake. Just say, "I'm sorry. I was wrong." God will forgive you.

An exciting thing to remember is that the limpet clings to the rock. Not only do you cling to God, He holds you tight. You are doubly safe.

When King David sinned, he felt separated from God. He writes about it in Psalm 2:3,4 "When I kept my sin to myself, I seemed to grow old, and all day long my heart groaned inside me. Day and night, I was under conviction and my strength slipped away as if it were a hot summer day. Then I decided to confess my sin to you and right what was wrong..."

Before David admitted his mistakes to God, He felt miserable. Guilt weighed him down. It threatened to separate him from God, but when He received God's gift of forgiveness, he felt joy again.

When you receive God's forgiveness, all the guilt that weighs you down, and loosens your hold on

Jesus, will disappear. The next time Satan hits you with a temptation, he will go away defeated because you know how to say no. You know how to stay connected just like the hundreds of limpets that hold on to the rocks along California's coast. You know how to tighten your grip on Jesus, your safe Rock.

### Discussion Questions

- What kind of power does a limpet have? How does this keep it safe?
- Jesus says that He is like a rock that we can cling to. What happens when we let go of Him?
- When the limpet let go of the rock, a seagull was able to knock it off and eat it. When we make a mistake, or let go of Jesus, what should we immediately do?

Sea Otters eating in a bed of Giant Kelp.

## Chapter 16
# Anchored

Thelma and I followed a narrow path that followed the edge of the cliffs that dropped off into the Great Pacific Ocean just south of Morrow Bay on California's Highway One. A great expanse of gold California Poppies spread out before us. Their waxy petals rippled in the sea breeze that wafted across the meadow. The cliffs wore a wig of thick grass. I imagined that the poppies created a spring bonnet for the cliffs to wear in its green hair.

We found a place in the grass and sat down. I dropped my backpack to the ground and pulled out a sketchpad and pencil. I drew a picture showing how the cliffs looked like large fingers jutting out into the ocean.

"Just look at this. You won't believe it," Thelma said, standing up.

"There are big holes in the sides of these cliffs."

I opened my plant press and arranged the stem and gold petals of a poppy on a sheet of white paper, then laid another sheet on top.

"Are you going to look?" she called.

I could hear the excitement in her voice changing to impatience as she walked off along the path at the edge of the cliff.

Getting the plant press put back together and tightening the straps took just a moment more. I stood up and gathered binoculars, bird books, and collecting gear and stuffed them into my pack.

"There are giant caves that I want to explore." She called out, not waiting for me to catch up.

I slung my pack over my back and ran down the narrow path.

"What's all the excitement about?" I teased as I arrived at her side.

"Just look at that," She shouted over the crashing of the waves.

"Wow," I exclaimed, staring at the opening in the finger of a tall cliff.

"That's what I've been trying to tell you. What do you think?"

"I think we ought to get down there and check them out."

We followed a trail through the grass until it ended at the edge of one of the cliff's fingers.

"The ocean is right below us," Thelma said, looking over the side of the steep cliff. "I don't see a way down."

"Let's try going down this rocky ravine." I pointed to a gully that ran like a dry stream bed to the beach below. We hadn't gone 20 feet when we stopped. "Oh, no," I cried. "Our way is blocked by a chain-link fence."

"What's it doing way out here?" Thelma groaned.

"That spot is big enough for us to squeeze under,"

I said, pointing to a wide place beneath the fence. "The rain must have washed the dirt away."

We both wiggled under the fence and picked our way over the rocks, not stopping to rest until we reached the sandy beach below.

A continuing series of brown fingers of land protruded into the rambunctious waves. Some of them reached several hundred feet seaward. We could see openings in their walls that led to more tiny beaches.

"Look at that," Thelma shouted. "The sea has carved two openings like huge arches into the stone."

"Can we get through the arches without being washed out to sea?" I called.

"I think we can," Thelma said. "The surf only reaches a bit past the openings. We can make a dash for it, between waves."

We headed for the arches. "They have to be 15 feet high," I said as I ran splashing in the wet sand, through the arch, and into the half-moon beach beyond.

We both stopped short and stared at the walls of the cliff.

"Caves!" we said at the same time, looking at the holes that disappeared in the darkness.

"I wonder how deep they go into the cliff?" I ventured, not certain that I really wanted to know.

"The only way we'll know is to go in them," Thelma suggested.

We looked at each other. "Of course," she added, "I don't want to become a human racquetball slammed around inside a dark cave by some wild wave."

"Just stay put a minute," I suggested. "Watch to see how far the water plunges into those openings."

We watched several waves hit the sand and creep

up the slanted beach into the caves.

"Let's make a run for it on the return flow of water, and take a quick look inside. If there's dry sand inside the cave, it means the edges of the waves don't reach to the back of the cave," I said. "It might be safe to explore for a few seconds."

When the surf pulled back, we ran to the entrance and peered inside. At least half of the sandy floor seemed dry so we cast a quick glance about us. A great heap of kelp lay strewn about the floor, told us that at high tides the sea did reach into the back corners of the cave.

"That's enough," Thelma said. "Let's go!"

I gave the kelp a kick to see if anything interesting lay hidden beneath it, then followed her to the entrance. As soon as the next wave retreated, we nearly stumbled over each other getting back to safer ground.

We made our way back up to the cliff tops and walked along their zigzag edges for a mile or so. At

A stalk of Giant Kelp.

this point they had become shorter, only reaching a dozen feet above the water. We lay down on the grass and rested.

"What's all that green stuff," Thelma asked, pointing to what looked like a blanket covering the

sea.

"That's Giant Kelp," I said. "And it's full of sea otters!" I screamed in excitement. "There must be more than twenty of them."

Thelma turned over and reached for her field glasses.

"Look at that large brown otter to your extreme right. He just dove under and came up with a Black Abalone," I shouted over the noise of crashing waves.

We watched as the otter floated on its back surrounded by the strands of kelp. It grabbed a chunk of white abalone meat and crammed it into its mouth. We laughed. In the middle of his meal, he rolled over, landing on his back again. The otter hung onto the shell and allowed the bits of meat and refuse to float away with the rippling water. Then it went right on snacking on the abalone. When it emptied the shell, the otter rolled over and dumped it into the sea. We watched the shell sink to the bottom.

"So that explains the empty abalone shells I sometimes see on the beach," Thelma said.

The rest of the day we watched the otters dive below the surface, kicking their powerful hind paddles. They seemed to eat at certain times, just like humans. Between feeding times, they enjoyed playing and swimming together. Throughout the day, we saw the otters rubbing their paws over their thick fur.

"They preen almost like birds do," Thelma observed.

"They're just trapping thousands of tiny air bubbles inside their fur. God taught them to do that."

"That's a weird way to stay warm and dry," Thelma

commented.

"I noticed that they eat a lot of abalones and sea urchins. It takes lots of calories every day to keep an otter full and warm." I answered.

Near sunset, we saw the otters settle down a bit. They spent extra time preening their fur. One by one, they began to roll over and over in the water. The long strands of kelp wrapped around their bodies until it was hard to see the exact shape of the sea otters.

"In all their antics and feeding activities they never leave the kelp beds," Thelma observed. "Now they're wrapping up in it. Why do they do that?"

"So they won't float out to sea when the tide changes," I answered, realizing that kelp was a fantastic plant. "Kelp doesn't have roots. A clump of root-like tentacles grows on the end of every stem. Scientists call this clump a Hold Fast. It acts like roots, and anchors the kelp to rocks on the sea floor."

"I've read that Giant Kelp grows very fast," Thelma said. "Sometimes it adds two feet a day until it reaches more than 200 feet."

"That means you could almost see it grow," I said, imagining the whole mass getting longer as I stared at it.

"The wrinkled 'leaves' that stick out along the stems look like rubber," Thelma remarked.

"Those are blades," I said. "Do you see the small oval bulbs that grow by each blade?"

"Yes. They look like green grapes."

"They aren't for eating," I laughed. "Think of them as little balloons filled with air. They grow along the kelp to keep the whole plant afloat."

"Wow!" Thelma said. "Just imagine popping all

those balloons. The whole mass of Giant Kelp would fall to the bottom of the sea in great heaps."

We both laughed.

As the sun passed behind the horizon and the sky grew dim, the otters settled into their kelp blankets and slept.

"It's wonderful," I sighed. "God gave them kelp beds to slosh in."

"And anchored blankets so they won't drift out to sea or smash against the rocky shore," Thelma added.

"The kelp also hides them from enemies, I said. "No wonder they sleep peacefully."

I stared at the brown lumps the otters made in the floating green beds.

"God is my Giant Kelp," I whispered. "I want to be all wrapped up in His love."

Thelma looked at me, then at the kelp. "Yes, we need something to wrap up in, too. We don't want to be without an anchor, so the currents of sin can catch us and thrash us about in the wild sea."

"That's a good object lesson," I said.

We watched the otters slosh until the darkness hid them from view.

"I hope I carry this picture with me forever," Thelma said as we climbed up the trail that led to our car.

Later, as we settled into our warm beds, I thought about those otters floating in their kelp beds. "The sea otter has the Giant Kelp, and I have God," I said. Then I fell asleep.

What do you want to wrap up in? You have choices. You could choose money, drugs, power, being popular, alcohol or even your own talents. You have to choose something that will give you safety and security.

Choose God, the true Giant Kelp. You will know the wonderful life of being wrapped up in His love. He promises you peace, friendship and the joy of a useful life.

The Bible says in Ephesians 1:7, "We have been redeemed by His blood and forgiven our sins, according to God's rich grace."

Accepting the free gift of God's forgiveness and wrapping up in His love will anchor you safely so that no power can remove you from Him. Now that's good news!

## Discussion Questions

- How do Sea Otters keep from drifting out to sea when they sleep at night?
- What do I mean when I say, "Jesus is my Giant Kelp?"
- Why don't we have to worry that each time we make a mistake, Jesus will stop loving us?

# Part 9

## I Made a Mistake

*Temptation*

The vast mud flats, at low tide, are home to many creatures.

## Chapter 17
# *Trapped in the Mud*

Day after day the sun rose in the January sky, only to be covered by gray clouds until darkness claimed the sky at evening time. Freezing rain pelted Maryland's grass-bare ground. I read through every dive magazine in my library, organized my shells, and dreamed of slithering along a coral reef off some distant island.

Finally, one bleak morning, I called my friend Martha.

"Let's get into the car and drive south until we find the sunshine. I feel like I'm frozen in gloom," I said.

"Great idea," she said, hanging up.

We packed our bathing suits, grabbed our shell collecting gear, and wiggled into coats. The chilled air snatched at us as we ran for the car and jumped in. We slammed the doors behind us and I started the car. It felt good to speed south along highway 95 toward Florida. Eight gray hours later we burst into the sun.

"Where are we?" Martha asked. "The sun is shining."

"It's Myrtle Beach," I said, parking the car just a few feet from the ocean and jumping out. Martha leaped out and stood beside me. The sun shone down. It reached warm fingers deep inside us, melting away our gloom.

"Myrtle Beach looks good," I said, wishing that I stood on some Caribbean shore instead, but glad to stand beside the sea. I threw off the jacket I'd worn all the way from Maryland.

"At least, the sun is shining," Martha said, turning her face up to catch the warmth.

"Nice day to be out," a lady said. She sat in the sand near our car, hunched up inside an oversized sweater.

We're from Maryland," we said together. "It feels so good to see the sunshine again," I added.

"Did you know there is a wildlife park south of town?" she asked. "It's a great place to snoop around. The marsh attracts lots of ducks and water birds."

We jotted down the directions, jumped into the car and headed south.

Beyond the parking lot, a wooden walkway jutted out over the marshy area that stretched between us and the sea. We followed it in the direction of the beach, passing two men who stared out over the marsh through twin sets of binoculars. They motioned to us. "Look at the wild geese," they said. We stopped and focused our binoculars on the geese. The joy of seeing God's creatures filled my heart and began to chase away the gloom.

We spent the next two hours standing on the wooden walkway watching wild ducks and Canada geese paddle their way over the smooth water. "That winter water doesn't bother them," Martha said, shaking her head.

"And they don't even need a wetsuit," I answered.

"This is more like it," Martha sighed. "But, I'm ready for a walk on the sandy shore and some wave watching."

"All right," I agreed, turning and scanning the marsh behind me. The soggy land spread out to the horizon like a thick, brown blanket. Tufts of long grass stuck up here and there.

"What are those?" I shouted to Martha, focusing on three tiny brown shells that clung to the blades of grass sticking out of the mud near the edge of the walkway.

"Shells!" Martha shouted. "They're only four feet away." Her eyes danced with excitement. "You could get them," she added.

"Why me?" I said, already reaching toward the shells. But no matter how far I stretched myself out over the wooden railing, I couldn't reach the shells. I tried to pull the tall grass toward me so I could grab the tiny treasures, but I just couldn't reach them.

"Lie down on your stomach," Martha suggested.

I lay down on the walkway, hung off the side and stretched forward, but they still sat beyond my reach.

"I'll hold your feet so you can stretch just a little more," Martha offered. "I think you've almost got them."

*This isn't a good idea,* I thought. I ignored my thoughts because I wanted those shells.

Our new plan didn't work, but neither of us wanted to give up the idea of owning a new kind of shell.

"I think I'll lower myself off the walkway and

hang by my hands. I can put one foot on a rock or hard place. The water is really shallow. I'll be able to reach forward a bit more and get those shells," I said.

"Are you sure you should try that?" Martha asked.

"You want those shells, don't you," I retorted. "I can do this."

I pulled off my socks and shoes and rolled up my pink sweatpants.

"Be ready to grab me if I start to sink," I instructed.

I saw Martha wring her hands as I eased over the edge of the walkway and lowered myself into the shallow water and mud. Black mud crept up my ankles.

"It's cold!" I screamed.

"Can you reach the shells?" Martha asked, ignoring my complaint.

I hung on, feeling around in the mud for a firm place to put my foot.

"The mud's so squishy. I can't find a foothold," I moaned. Suddenly my arms felt weak. "I can't hang on much longer," I said, looking up at Martha. "Maybe you should grab me and try to pull me out before I sink down anymore."

"Is there a cross bar beneath the walkway?" Martha asked. "You could jam your foot or knee onto it and push yourself up."

I dragged one foot out of the mud and fumbled around under the walkway.

"There's nothing here," I cried.

Cold mud oozed up around my knees and my hands began to lose their grip on the walkway.

"I'll take one of your hands and pull you up," Martha said, getting down on her knees and reaching out toward me. "You hold on with the other one."

*143*

Suddenly I didn't want to let go of one hand so she could get a hold of me.

"No, you're not strong enough to get me out," I said. "If I slip lose, I'll fall flat on my back. The thick mud will suck me under."

"Could you swim to shore?" Martha asked.

"No!" I shouted. "There's not enough water on top of the mud to float me."

For long moments, we stared at each other.

"I've got to get out," I wailed.

I thought of sliding my hands along the walkway toward the shore that lay about a hundred feet away, but knew I couldn't hang on long enough.

*I've gotten myself into a real mess,* I thought. *But there must be some way to escape.*

Cold fear crept into my brain. Tears slid down my cheeks and dropped to the mud below. I just hung on and waited for the moment the freezing mud would swallow me up.

"You need help, fast." Martha gasped, looking at my face.

She closed her eyes. I could see her lips moving. "Help us find a way, God," I heard her say.

"God is going to help us," Martha said, looking up. "We should have asked Him sooner."

Suddenly she flung herself down onto the walkway, hooking her feet on the far edge of the wooden slats. I watched numbly as she hung her arms over the side of the walkway and made a sling with her hands by interlacing her fingers together.

"Try to get one foot free of the mud and jam it into my hands," she said. "I'll give you a yank and pull you up."

"I know my fingers don't look very strong," she said, guessing what I was thinking. "Even a slight yank might dislodge you and set you free. God will help us."

Using all my strength, I twisted my foot and then pulled hard. The mud loosened its hold on me. My leg shot out of the mud and into Martha's hand.

"Now!" Martha yelled.

She screamed and yanked. I flung myself forward, slithering, on my stomach, under the railing and across the walkway. For a second, I didn't move. I just clung to the hard, dry, wooden planks beneath me.

Martha laughed. I laughed. We struggled to our feet. Then we thanked God for helping me get out of that mud trap alive.

Together we headed toward the beach beyond the marsh hoping to find a public washroom. Clumps of mud fell from my sweat suit and hit the walkway leaving a trail behind me. A couple with binoculars slung around their necks passed. They stared at us.

"We must look terrible," Martha said.

"I don't care," I retorted. "It feels so good to be free of that mud."

The path led up over a bluff and ended near the beach.

"Water!" I shouted, spotting a building with a faucet sticking through the wooden wall. I ran ahead of Martha, leaving splotches of mud behind me.

"You mean you haven't had enough water?" Martha called after me.

I grabbed the faucet handle and turned it on. A thin stream of water dribbled out. I began to scrub and scrape the mud from my body beginning with my hands and face. My skin got red and I shivered with cold.

"It doesn't look like you are getting very clean,"

Martha said. "Maybe you could rinse off in the sea."

"I'd freeze if I did that," I wailed, realizing my trouble wasn't over yet.

"I'll get some dry clothes and a beach towel from the car," Martha said. "Now I know why you always carry extra clothes," she teased as she disappeared over the bluff.

I flung myself over a dune and soaked up the warmth that the sun had left behind, mixing the mud and the sand together. While I waited for Martha, God spoke to my heart.

"This is the way it is when you get stuck in the mud of sin. You think you can handle it yourself. You think you're strong, but you're weak. You can't save yourself. Call on me. I'm strong."

"I also know that I can't clean myself up," I whispered.

Martha popped up over the dune. She saw the sand I'd added to myself.

"Let's get a motel room," she said. "You're going to need lots of warm water and soap."

"I can't get into the car like this," I cried. "I just have to get some of this off."

We both turned and looked at the sea.

"There isn't any other way," I said heading for the water.

I fell into the surf, screaming and shaking from the cold. When I ran out, Martha wrapped me in a big beach towel. We headed for the car.

At our room, at last, I tore off the pink sweat suit and threw it into the trash, knowing I could never get it clean again. I stood under the shower and let it pour over me until every bit of mud disappeared down the drain.

Two hours later we sat beside the sea once more.

I felt clean and dry as we watched the water pile up, then tumble to the shore. The sun danced and played with the waves.

"I almost died today," I said to Martha who lay sprawled out beside me on the warm sand. "I'm glad you were there and that God helped us."

Martha grinned. "You looked awful," she said. "But I was so happy to see you come up out of that sludge, I almost hugged you."

Suddenly I imagined how I looked and smelled when Martha dragged me out of the marsh. I knew why she hauled me off to a hot shower. It felt good to have a friend that cared for me even in my muddy condition.

If you're in big trouble like I was, you'll be glad to know there's really someone out there who cares about you in your sinful condition. If you think I looked and smelled awful, just imagine how sin makes you appear to God. Call for help. He will hear you and pull you right out of the mud and into the sunshine of His love.

His love, like a cascading warm shower, will rinse away the slime of sin. Imagine it! Like fresh rain, God's love and forgiveness will pour over you. You can feel it washing you from head to toe. It flows through your hair and over your head cleansing your mind and giving it new thoughts. It washes over your eyes giving you the ability to see the things God is teaching you in a new way. Down it flows over you putting new and positive power-words into your mouth.

Imagine the love and forgiveness of God washing over your body, removing every dark stain of muddy sin and helping you become healthy and strong. It floods over your feet, giving you the desire to walk in His way.

Now you can see why He calls Himself the Water of Life. You get the picture, from my adventure, that He alone can wash you clean. So don't try to rescue yourself and try to clean the sin off. You won't have any better luck than I did at that faucet nor in the frigid surf.

I know that God is just waiting to do all this for you because it says so in Isaiah 65:24. "Before they call, I will answer. While they are still speaking, I will respond."

And you will find a fantastic promise in 1 John 1:7. "The blood of Jesus Christ will cleanse you from all sin." He died and shed His blood to make forgiveness available to you. He IS the Water of Life, well able to wash you clean.

Martha and I returned to the nature park. We walked on the walkway especially constructed to keep us out of the mud. I stayed on the walkway! I stayed clean and dry.

### Discussion Questions

- I tried so hard to pull myself out of the mud. What did I do that finally made my escape possible?
- How did I clean myself up?
- When we fell into the mud of sin, Satan thought Jesus would throw us away. What did Jesus do instead?

## Chapter 18

# *Stuck*

I stood beside George and Thelma in the bow of their new cabin cruiser. It sat tied to the dock that jutted out from Plantation Key, a tiny island in a chain of small pieces of land off Florida's southern tip. We gazed at the rumpled surface of the sea. It sloped in every direction, setting the ship dancing like a leaping dolphin.

"The wind has died down," Thelma said. "Maybe the water will settle down soon."

"We've waited two days already," George moaned. He ran one hand along the teak trim that decorated the boat.

"I'm willing to give it a try," I said, gazing at the thrashing sea.

It took less than ten minutes to reach the dive site. We suited up and lingered only a moment on the dive platform before throwing ourselves into the water. Both of us disappeared beneath the surface and popped back up. Thelma waved from the boat that heaved and dipped with the rough sea. *It just might be calmer deeper down,* I thought, reaching out and grabbing the anchor line and sinking toward the bottom. George sank down just a few feet ahead of me. I couldn't see a foot in front of me nor in any direction. Suddenly my right fin hit the sand. I swirled about searching for George in the murky water, but he had disappeared.

Suddenly I spotted a lime-green line that looked like a snake lying on the sandy bottom. I tried to jerk myself away. When the line stood up, my heartbeat slowed to normal. *That is just the green stripe on George's dive suit,* I thought. *But why is he crumpled up on the sand? He must have reached the bottom sooner than he expected, and hit it.*

I clung to the anchor line and looked around. *I'm close to the reef, but can't see a single coral head or fish swishing past,* I thought. *And I can't see George. Diving is about seeing, and I can't see.* I gave the signal for "going up." *Surely George will catch my signal.* My body slowly rose to the surface and I flung myself over the back of the boat. A moment later, George arrived at the ladder.

"It's a mess down there," I gasped. "Visibility isn't more than three feet," I said to George as he climbed into the boat.

We each removed our gear in silence. I could sense George's disappointment. I felt bad, too. I usually stayed down as long as possible because I loved being on the reef, but this time, it felt good to be the first one out.

"Let's find a place to shell," Thelma suggested.

George nodded and scanned the sea. "The water around the keys is so shallow that I'm sure we can find a sand bar out here somewhere," he said, a bit of enthusiasm leaking into his voice.

"Look!" I shouted pointing toward shore.

"That's a big one," George said, smiling. "Let's go."

We sped away toward the sand bar. When we reached it, George anchored next to the bar and Thelma and I jumped overboard.

We scrambled over the wet surface of the sand, picking up shells, and poking at strange creatures stranded by the retreating water. I smiled as I looked out over acres of sand just waiting to be investigated. *So many treasures and so little time*, I thought.

Too soon, the sun slid down onto the horizon. I stopped playing tag with a crab and looked at the boat. George waved at us.

"Come on," he called. "We should try to get to the dock before dark."

Thelma and I sloshed through the shallow water and climbed into the boat. "You're right. It's getting dark, fast," she said. "We better head for the harbor."

We stored our bags of shells below deck. George got the boat ready and started up the motor. I held on, waiting for the boat to speed away from the edge of the sand bar that seemed to be getting bigger all the time. *I wish I could stay out longer and take a look at the far end of the bar*, I thought. *More sand is being exposed every minute.*

George gunned the motor again, but we didn't move. He fiddled with some levers. We waited. The sun kept lowering itself into the sea.

"Are we leaving soon?" Thelma asked, looking at the darkening sky.

"We're stuck!" George announced.

Thelma and I looked at each other, considering

several possible fates.

"I think I can get us going if you both get out and push," George said.

*That's not going to help,* I thought. *You push cars on dry land, not boats stuck in the sand.*

I looked at my collecting gear sitting on the floor of the boat. It bulged with treasures. *Hey,* I thought, *he got us out here, and we found lots of great shells. If he needs me to push the boat, I'll push.*

"OK," I said, climbing overboard.

"There's stuff out there in that dark water," Thelma mumbled as she climbed onto the dive platform and jumped into the shallow water. "They might sample our legs."

"I know," I said, jamming my feet into the sand and heaving against the boat with my right shoulder.

The boat didn't move.

"We've got a problem," George said, sweeping his gaze along the shore through the darkening sky.

Thelma and I stared at each other.

"There seems to be more sand sticking up from the sea than when we first arrived," I said. "The boat is sitting in very shallow water. Hand me my snorkel and mask, George."

I pushed my mask into place and ducked down into the water, looking at the bottom of the boat, then stood up, pushing my mask back and spitting out my snorkel.

"We're stuck all right," I said.

George looked at the darkening sky and the disappearing shoreline. "I'm not sure I can find our little spot along the shore once it gets dark," he muttered. We stood staring out into the night, each lost in thought. A few lights flickered on along the coast.

"Will we be stuck out here all night?" Thelma asked.

*That wouldn't be so bad,* I thought. *It might be a nice adventure. I could scamper over the sand bar with a flashlight.*

"Look! A sailboat," Thelma shouted. "I thought we were the last ones out on the ocean."

"It's moving toward us on its way into one of the little harbors," I cried, feeling a bit disappointed.

"Ahoy, mates," a man called as his boat neared us. "Need some help?"

"No, everything's fine," George shouted back. "Thanks."

*George,* I thought. *It's not fine. Remember the sand that's up around the boat holding us fast. Remember the sun that's disappearing so we can't see the entrance to the harbor.*

"He'd never be able to pull us lose," George said, looking at our stunned faces. "This is a big boat. Only something very powerful could free us."

No one spoke as the sky turned dark blue, then black. No one wanted to suggest calling the harbor patrol. We knew they'd charge more than $1,000 to haul us off the bar and guide us into the harbor.

*What comes next?* I wondered as darkness settled around us.

Two hours passed. George fiddled with the boat's motor while each of us sat silently trying to think of some wild rescue plan. One by one, a few more lights popped on all along the shore, but we couldn't see which ones marked our harbor.

Several hours passed as I looked out over the sandbar, watching the water slosh. It washed against the edges of the sandbar, moving closer and closer toward the middle. The great stretch of sand seemed to shrink before my eyes. Water trickled over the flat surface, filling small depressions, making them into pools.

Suddenly I leaped to my feet. "We don't have a problem," I shouted.

"What?" George and Thelma said together.

"What is the one thing strong enough to lift us off this sandbar?" I asked looking into their faces.

"The tide!" Thelma shouted. She looked at the sandbar and back at George.

"The tide is changing. It's moving in so the water will get deeper!" George shouted.

We laughed. We stopped worrying and enjoyed the cool evening, waiting while the tide moved in. It covered more and more of the sand bar. The tide lifted us up like a strong hero and wiggled us free of the sand. Soon we drifted out into the deeper water to the powerful tide, we were like a mere piece of straw.

Once free from the sand, we sped away from the sandbar. George pointed a large spotlight at the land and we passed along as close as possible to the shore. Suddenly we spotted our small harbor. It felt good to see that familiar dock waiting for us.

The returning tide was the only force strong enough to unstick our boat from the sand. And there's only One powerful enough to unstick you if you get caught on the sand bar of sin. His name is God. He's your Hero. He flung the stars into space. He called the sea into being with a word. His strength established the power of the tides that moves entire oceans.

First, you must recognize your mistake or the poor choice that got you stuck in the first place. Then, just call on God. Don't be afraid. Be smart.

He'll send a flood of help that will lift you right out of your trouble. Then you can speed safely into the harbor of His love.

Hebrews 1:3 tells you that, "He holds all things in the universe together by the power of His word. He single-handedly saved us from the power of sin and is now seated on the right hand of the mighty God of the universe."

Maybe you think it was funny for Thelma and me to try to push that boat. We didn't have that kind of strength. But just imagine how foolish it is when you try to un-stick yourself from a bad habit, or sin, or trouble you're in. You just can't do it. Realize that; ask for help, and watch the power of God set you free.

Let me tell you about a power in your body that I just learned about. It's called, Laminin. Go ahead and Google it. You will find that Laminin is a protein molecule that works like glue. It's actually called a protein adhesion molecule. It takes the shape of a very miniature cross and there are millions of them throughout your body. They keep you from flying apart. They are the power of God keeping you together in the midst of all your life's adventures and situations.

God invented these tiny specks of life and allowed scientists to discover them, to assure you that He is well able to hold your life together through all sorts of situations. He not only rescues you, but He is your personal Hero.

The tide, powered by God's moon, can lift a boat because it moves the sea in and out. That's great! But how much greater is the power of your Hero. He's your Laminin. And you need him right now.

## Discussion Questions

- Nature helps us understand the truth about Jesus. How did the moon help us get free from the sand?
- How is Jesus like the powerful moon?
- Why can't we get ourselves out of the mud of sin?

# Part 10

I Belong to the Dive Master

~~~~~~~~~~~~~~~~~~~~~~~~~~~~~~~~~~~~~~

*Walking With Jesus*

A Peacock Flounder escaping from the curious author.

## Chapter 19
# The Fantastic Flounder

For three days January's cold wind blew over the surface of the sea that surrounded Marathon Key. It built up walls of water digging out deep trenches in the sand. It reached fingers down into the bay and flung waves against the beach. It howled in the treetops and sent boat flags dancing.

"I can't swim in this stuff," I cried, noticing that even the gulls had left the beach.

On the fourth morning, I awoke to silence and dashed to the window. A pale-yellow sun rested on the horizon. I jumped into my bathing suit and ran to the water's edge. The sea lay still, glistening in the morning sunbeams. I waded into the water, attached my snorkel to my mask, and dove in. My friends, George and Thelma, joined me.

"Looks like pea soup," I said, standing up.

We shook our heads and returned to our rooms. We threw down our mask and fins and grabbed collecting bags.

# The Fantastic Flounder

"That wind and wild sea have tossed up some shells somewhere," Thelma declared, a bit of enthusiasm creeping into her voice. "Let's go look around."

We managed to find some good shells, but George and I longed for the reef.

The next day the water looked calmer so we grabbed our dive gear. Thelma gathered a lunch and shelling equipment. We tossed everything into the boat and headed out to the reef that lay four miles from the island.

"We just have to give it a try," George said.

I wondered what diving in pea soup might be like. *How could we see the reef?* How could we see each other well enough to stay together? And what about those sharks? They would see us. I felt sure of that. But I wanted to dive so I pushed all fearful thoughts away.

When we arrived at the reef, two other boats were anchored to the buoys. The water rose and fell in large swells and my stomach churned as we suited up.

"This isn't a good day to dive," I said to George. Neither of us stopped putting on our gear. We glanced at the water. It looked milky. I fell over twice trying to get my wetsuit on, and noticed that my dive buddy struggled too, and retched once or twice. *He feels like I do,* I thought.

George gave me the OK signal and jumped off the boat. He started toward the sea floor. I held my right hand over my mask and took the "giant leap" that I had learned as a student diver, feeling the cold water surround me. In an instant, I surfaced and headed for the anchor line. Instead of going down head first, I decided to go down the anchor line slowly and clear my ears as I moved deeper and deeper into the water.

*I can't see ten feet ahead,* I thought. *This is weird.*

The reef looked like a gray monster in the murky distance. I checked my depth gauge and realized I must be near the bottom. I couldn't see the sand or any corals, so I just hung there staring.

George had disappeared into the fog of sand that filled the sea. I swirled in a complete circle, searching the water for his blue dive suit. *If I let go of this anchor line, I'll never find it again,* I thought. *I can't see the reef and can hardly see my dive buddy.* As much as I wanted to dive, it didn't seem like a good idea, I gave George the signal for, "going up" and began to go hand over hand up the anchor line. I felt cold and couldn't see anything, even my own feet. *This dive is over,* I thought, slowly ascending to the boat. We sat silently as we sped back to our dock.

Later in the afternoon, I stood staring at the murky water for a long time.

*Maybe I could snorkel in a protected part of the bay,* I thought, leaving my place in front of the window, grabbing my snorkel gear, and heading out the door.

I eased myself into the water and sloshed about like a cork. *This isn't going to work,* I thought, *but how can I get out without seeing even one cowrie shell?* I turned a few rocks, but that just stirred up more sediment until I lay in a white cloud unable to see anything.

Just as I moved toward shore, and prepared to climb out, I noticed the round shape of a fish. It lay still on the white sand not more than three feet beneath me. Two plump, round eyes sat perched close together atop its flat head. I swallowed the laughter that threatened to burst out when I saw that each eye rolled in its socket, working independently of the other. I could see through the murky water the iridescent purple rings that decorated its body.

"It's a Peacock Flounder," I shouted into my snorkel. "And I'm so close to it." I laughed again.

The flounder looked up and flattened itself into the sand in an attempt to hide from me, the hovering monster.

I remembered that flounders start life much like any other fish, with eyes on each side of its head. But, by some miracle that God invented, all that changes. The Peacock Flounder lies on one side,

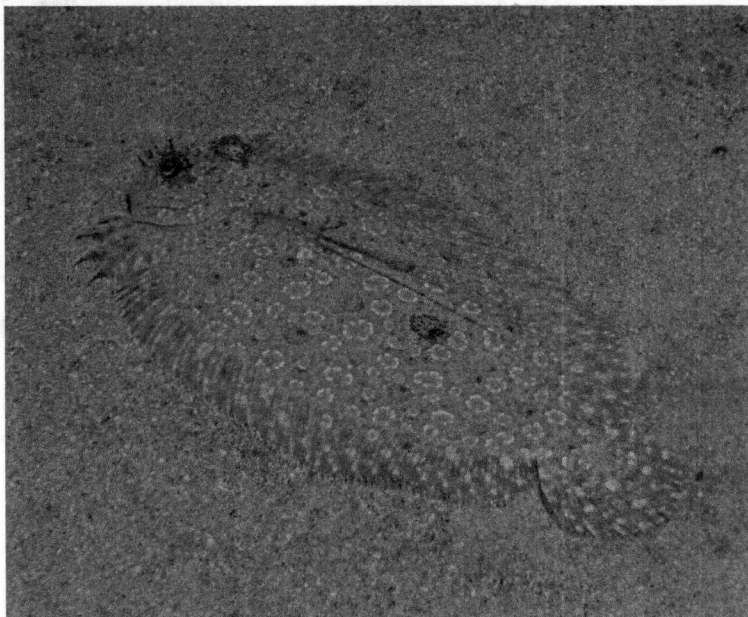

A Peacock Flounder using his camouflage gifts. ©Reggie Thomas

flattens out, and moves one eye to join the eye that faces up. Both eyes are now side by side on the top of the fish, and they both bug out on the same side of the face. Weird!

I also remembered that flounders don't go dashing about after food. They wait until the food comes to them. *They must be very patient,* I thought. But I didn't feel that patient. I wanted action.

*I wonder how fast a flounder can slither along the sand,* I thought. *If it gets scared, will it dart off like a floating pancake?* I waved my hand in the water right over its head, feeling sure the flounder would flee at top speed. To my surprise, it looked up at me and simply lay close to the sandy sea floor. I waved both hands, but the flounder didn't move.

Next, I pressed the button on my dive knife. It almost jumped out of the scabbard that I had strapped to my leg. I waved it back and forth near the flounder. The flounder didn't move. It didn't take off. It simply changed color to match the exact colors of the sand around it. The flounder stuck with its hiding place in the sand and almost disappeared from sight.

I felt amazed. *This fish obeys the voice in its head and stays put,* I thought. *Any other fish would jet away. I wonder what it does do when a real danger threatens it? Maybe I don't look very frightening. I think I'll see if I can make it panic.*

I took off one pink fin and slipped it beneath the flounder's body, flipping it into the water column. If a fish can look surprised, it did. In an instant that fish darted away from me, staying very close to the sand.

*Now I can chase him,* I thought. *I will be faster than the fish.* But, to my complete surprise, the flounder dove into the soft sand not ten feet away. It shook itself until white sand covered it. That fish almost disappeared from my sight, blending into the colors of its surroundings. "Wow!" I whispered into my snorkel.

I hovered over the flounder, watching it for as

long as I could stand the cold water, but after a few minutes, my lips turned blue and my body shivered. *I have to leave you, little flounder,* I thought. *You are very brave and smart. Thanks for making me laugh.*

I thought about the obedient flounder as I staggered out of the water and headed for my hotel room. I wondered how it managed to make itself sit still and not panic even while a big predator like me hovered above it. It glanced at me until it realized that an enemy threatened its very life. Then the flounder gazed at the sand. The cells in its eyes told its brain the colors of the sand. Then the cells in its skin flipped over until they mimicked the exact colors in the sand. *That sand covers the flounder and hides it from enemies,* I thought, *and God gives it the power to change color.*

So, the flounder glances at the enemy and then stares at its savior, the sand. The secret of the flounder is much like your own secret. Be aware, glance at your enemy, but don't stare long enough to become discouraged. Gaze at the One who saves you. You will become more like Him as you focus on Him just as the flounder changes color while it gazes at the sand. What the sand is to the Peacock Flounder, God is to you.

Don't panic! You've chosen God to be your "Dive Master." Follow Him as you move through the reef of life. Don't let an enemy scare you away from the One who will keep you safe.

Glance at the enemy and gaze at God. The flounder trusts this method of living and growing up in the reef.

Pray, choose to trust and obey. These are what keep you close to your Savior. The same God who placed the life-saving information into the head of every flounder, will put knowledge and power into your mind. This way you will grow and stay safe as you adventure through life.

**Discussion Questions**

- What does the brave flounder do to stay safe from predators?
- A Dive Master has lots of experience. It's his job to make sure every diver has a safe dive. How is Jesus like a Dive Master?

A Venus Tower is home to the tiny Spongecola Shrimp.

# Chapter 20
# Tower Power

Imagine, for a moment, that you're a Spongecola Shrimp. Your eyes pop open and you realize that you've just been born. You look at yourself and see that your body is nothing more than a speck of gelatin bobbing about in a great ocean. Legs, as thin as human hair, stick out from your sides.

You look around. You aren't floating on the surface where the sun paints the water gold. No sunbeams warm your back. You can't see the reef where rainbow colored fish swish past and sea fans nod into the current. You don't see any Moray Eels peeking green heads from dark crevices. You swirl about in the water and don't catch sight of a single living thing.

Suddenly a Gulper Fish, a snakelike creature with a head the size of a grapefruit, bursts out of the darkness. Its open mouth is ablaze with bioluminescent light and it flashes blue, yellow, white, and red lights at you. Terror seizes you. Your whole body shakes. Your heart cries out, "Is there no safe place for me to hide?" You feel helpless. Fear drives you to dive down as the predator soars past and disappears into the darkness. The flash of light it leaves behind becomes dim and you're alone.

You dive deeper and deeper into the blackness. At 5,000 feet you bump into a rock at the bottom of the sea. Then a voice speaks inside your brain. The voice tells you to go find the tower and get inside quickly. The voice is instinct, placed there by your Creator. You spin around in a full circle, searching for a tower.

Suddenly you see something fastened to a rock with silver threads called byssus threads. It looks like a tower. It stands twelve inches high and is as big around as a young sand dollar. It shines white against the blackness.

Scientists have named this object the Venus Tower, but you don't know that. You just see a delicate, mesh structure that looks like a miniature fisherman's net, starched and rolled up. As you stare at the glass-like woven threads of the tower, you think, *this is my safe place.*

Your tiny heart thumps as you head for the tower. Around and around you swim, but you don't see a door. It doesn't matter because you soon discover that you are so small that you can squeeze through any opening in the mesh walls. You poke your head into the tower, then your body and legs.

A delicious sense of safety floods over you. It feels so good to be safe. You swirl around in circles until you reach the top, then plunge to the bottom.

After all your adventures, you realize that you feel hungry. You wonder how you will find food if you stay in the tower.

Suddenly you see that tiny specks of food in the form of zooplankton and phytoplankton filtering through the tower's cracks. The sea currents wash them into your home and out again. You grab them as fast as you can and stuff them into your mouth.

Now you think, *I am safe and full. That's good. But, it's a bit lonely in here all by myself.* Your tiny eyes focus on something in the darkness beside you. It's another Spongecola Shrimp. You're not alone after all.

This is when your brain, no larger than the sharp end of a pin, tells you that everything you will ever need is right there in the tower. Your fear, your hunger, and loneliness float away on the sea current.

But you are not a Spongecola Shrimp. You're a human. You were cast, at birth, into a sin-darkened world. The predator, Satan, cruises the reef of your life. He is determined to destroy you. Fear drives you to search for a safe place. You see others building safe places because they're afraid, too. Some choose to trust in things that promise to make them feel safe, like money, security, status, education, talent, career, success, and even the heart of a friend. But as you watch, you discover that these things that promise security can crumble. You cry out, "Isn't there a safe place for me that I can trust?"

The resounding answer to your cry comes from God. "I am your safe place." The Bible tells you, in Proverbs 10:18, that you have a tower, too. It says, "The name of the Lord is a strong tower. The righteous run into it, and are safe."

Your Creator longs to erase your fear and loneliness. He has given you a safe place as real and beautiful as the tower He placed it in the depths of the sea for the Spongecola Shrimp. This safe place is

**169**

the heart of our Savior Jesus, and God our Father.

Jesus is like a strong tower. God sent Him to this earth to be a tower that cannot fall. How do I know this? Follow His story through the pages of the Bible and see for yourself.

From the cradle to the grave Jesus stood against the gale force of Satan's temptations and human plots. Nothing could destroy the One that God sent to be our Tower. Now He stands beside the throne of God pointing to the nail prints in His hands. The Prince of Peace, the Lamb that was slain, the Mighty King stands, a safe Tower, pure and glorious amid the darkness of sin.

Whenever I begin a new day, or return to the sea, I pause and imagine myself enclosed within the safety of my own Tower. Then, I go my way with a joy and peace I never thought possible because the presence of this Tower, Jesus, has erased fear and made me certain that I am never alone.

Discover Jesus, the Tower in whom you can find everything you will ever need. Discover His love. Make Him your Hero. Admit your guilt and understand your sin. Let Him change you into a new creature and become His partner. Ask Him for the power to live a life like His, full of love and kindness.

If you make a mistake, just say, "I'm sorry." He will fill you with joy because now you are part of His family. You belong to Him. When He comes again, He will take you home to live with Him forever.

Choose to trust the Tower that will never fall. Feel the safety of the Tower you run to, not from. The Spongecola Shrimp has its Venus Tower and you have Jesus. Now, nothing is left but for you to choose whether you will run to Him or not.

## *Triton's Treasure*

### Discussion Questions

- How does Jesus provide for the tiny Spongecola Shrimp so it doesn't have to live in fear?
- What does Jesus give me so I am able to dive into the sea without fear?
- When we choose Jesus, we become part of Family. How do you feel about being a part of His family?

# Treasures by the Sea
# Bonus Chapter

## Chapter 1

~~~~~~~~~~~~~~~~~~~~~~~~~~~~~~~~~~~~~~~~~

## Storm Clouds

# Treasures
by the
# Sea

Get set for adventure as Eric and Susan
discover exciting truths about God's love.

# Sally Streib

# Chapter 1
# Storm Clouds

Eric stood before the bedroom window and gazed out over the Chesapeake Bay. Black clouds rolled across the sky like tumble weeds driven by the wind. They piled into heaps until they blotted out the afternoon sun. Jagged fingers of lightening tore through the clouds and jabbed at the surging mass of dark water. The storm raged against the land like the dark thoughts that churned inside Eric's mind. All at once the clouds dumped their load of rain. It pounded against Eric's window.

"Eric. Are you in there?" Susan called. Before he could answer, his door flew open and Susan burst inside. She stood shivering in the darkened room.

He quickly brushed a stray tear from his cheek and struggled to gain control of his voice before he turned to face Susan.

"Are you afraid?" she asked.

"Of course not," Eric blurted. "I was just watching the storm, that's all."

"I'm scared," Susan said. She still hadn't moved

174

from the doorway. Lightening tore through the dark sky followed by a clap of thunder. Susan jumped. Eric grabbed the curtains and drew them across the window. He flopped down on the rug beside his bed.

"You can stay here if you want," he said, motioning for Susan to come in.

Susan flung herself onto Eric's bed. "I hate storms," she said.

She is scared of everything since Mother died, Eric thought.

"What's going to happen to us, Eric?"

"I don't know. But Dad is trying to work something out." He reached over and gave Susan an awkward pat on her shoulder.

"I wish I could be brave like you," Susan sobbed. "Don't you ever feel afraid?" She looked up at him.

He didn't want to lie to his twin sister, but how could he tell her how angry he felt.

"I don't want to go away, that's all," Eric said, banging his fist into the rug.

"Tell Father," Susan pleaded.

"That's easy for you to say. Besides, Father wouldn't listen."

Susan crawled off the bed and sat beside Eric. Neither spoke. The darkness wrapped itself around them.

"Eric! Susan! Where are you?"

"It's Father!" Eric said, jumping up. He opened the door. "We're in here."

Father appeared in the doorway. "Hey, why are you sitting in the dark?"

"I was just watching the storm. Susan was scared, so I pulled the curtains."

"We were talking, Father," Susan stood and turned to face her father.

# Storm Clouds

"I see," he said. "It looks very gloomy to me. Something you want to share?"

Susan gave Eric a this-is-your-chance-to-talk-to-him glance. Eric noticed the tired expression on his father's face. His eyes seemed dull and lifeless. Why did Mother have to die, he thought. Why did that old drunk have to hit her? I hate him. I hate him! Now my whole life is ruined. His thoughts crowded out the words he wanted to say.

"We don't want to be sent away, Father," Susan blurted.

"So that's it." He pulled his daughter close. "I know this isn't what we want. But for now, it's the best I can manage. Your Aunt Sally has agreed to let you live with her through the next school year until..."

"A whole year?" Eric groaned. "But Father..."

"I know, Eric. There's the baseball team. You won't be able to play this year. You'll miss your friends. But I'm swamped with details. I have to sell the house and finish my last year at the university. I just don't know how I can handle all this." He leaned forward, resting his head in his hands. The room filled up with silence.

"We can help," Susan said. "I can cook and clean the house."

"Susan," Father interrupted. "You and Eric are only twelve. No, it's final. I don't like this either, but for your sakes it's best. Aunt Sally is a good woman. She has a lovely home on the ocean, so you'll have everything you need there."

"We don't want everything," Eric was surprised to hear himself say. "We want you, Father."

Susan caught her breath. No one spoke for a long moment.

**176**

Father looked at Eric, then at Susan. "I see," he said. "You're afraid you'll lose me too."

He reached out toward them. "That will never happen."

Susan ran to her father and buried her head on his shoulder. Eric pressed against his other side, and the three clung together.

"I just don't know what else I can do," Father said, at last. "You understand, don't you?" his voice pleaded.

"Sure, Father." Eric nudged Susan.

"We'll be all right," Susan whispered, her voice quivering.

"Now, let's make the best of this." Father stood up and started for the door. "Why don't you wash up for supper?"

The door shut, and Eric looked at Susan. "See. It didn't do a bit of good to tell him how I felt," he grumbled.

"Maybe there just isn't anything else he can do," Susan reasoned. "We could try to understand."

"Sure," Eric said, his voice heavy with doubt.

During the next two days a silent gloom settled over the house. Eric brooded in his room and Father kept busy at the office. Susan spent hours wandering along the edge of the bay. She dug her toes into the golden sand and watched the sailboats skim over the water. She would miss the bay. Everything good was about to drain out of her life. Would she ever be happy again? Would Eric? She missed his teasing. He didn't laugh anymore. And he was always so grumpy. If only she could talk to Mother right now.

"I miss her so much." Susan sighed. A sea gull swooped down beside her. He plunged his bill into the wet sand and flew out over the bay.

# Storm Clouds

"I wish I could fly away like you," Susan called after him. She stood staring after the gull. "I wonder how far it is to God's house," she said out loud.

Another gull circled overhead, then landed on the water. His body bobbed over the gentle swells. Susan cupped her hands around her mouth. "Hey, Mr. sea gull, did God make you?" she yelled. "Is He real?"

The gull just floated along, not seeming to hear.

Oh, well, Susan thought, even if there is a real God who created everything, I don't think if I want to know Him. Didn't He let Mother die in that terrible car crash? Still . . .

"Do you always talk to the gulls?" Eric said, coming up behind her.

Susan jumped! "Do you have to scare a person?"

"Come on. Father is home early and wants to talk to us."

The twins walked silently up the beach and opened the back door to the kitchen. Father leaned against the cupboard, sipping a hot drink.

"Hi," he said. A smile played at the corners of his mouth. "Sit down, and let's eat."

Susan stared at the supper table. Potatoes, a roast, and salad sat in the middle of the table. Three places had been neatly set, and a flower poked a brave head from a small vase at the end of the table.

"You did all this?" she gasped.

"I certainly did," Father said proudly, wiping his hands on a towel. "We're going to celebrate."

"Celebrate what?" Eric asked.

"I have news," Father said. His eyes smiled. "It can wait until we eat, however."

"No," Susan shouted. "Tell us now, or I won't eat a bite." She tugged on her father's arm.

"You're an impossible impatient woman!" Father

178

teased. "I've worked something out with my boss and also with the university."

"OK! Wow!" Eric almost exploded with enthusiasm.

"Not so fast son." A firm tone crept into Father's voice and his smile faded a bit.

"First of all, I have to train my partner to take over my job. Second, I'll stay here and take the summer session at the university. Then I'll join you in California, working with the university's extension program. I believe I can graduate a year from now. When we return to Maryland for my finals, we can find a home that suits us."

"But we still have to stay with Aunt Sally all summer." Susan's voice was flat. She twisted her long brown braids together.

"That's true, Princess. But, we'll soon be together again." Susan flung her arms around Father's neck.

"That's what we want most," she cried, "We want to be together."

"I know that now," Father said.

"Well, Son, do you think you can live with that?"

"Sure, Father," Eric said. He felt disappointed, but three months seemed better than a whole year. Still, the whole thing made him uneasy. He didn't want to live in California anyway, much less with a spinster aunt he hardly knew.

Eric and Susan spent the next two weeks cleaning the house. Susan dusted and waxed floors until they shone. Eric washed every window. Dad pounded a sign into the front lawn. FOR SALE, the black letters shouted.

Soon they found themselves climbing aboard a giant 747 jet-powered airliner. Susan stared through the small window down at the Chesapeake Bay and the forests that soon gave way to farms ending at

**179**

the edge of the Mississippi River. She sighed. Their home on the Bay was now far behind her.

"Look at that," Eric said pointing out the small, oval window. "It's the Grand Canyon."

"And the desert," Susan said. Just when she thought the desert would go on forever, they flew over a great mountain range topped with snow. Ridges and valleys stretched as far as she could see. They looked different from the mountains of Maryland. Everything is going to be different, she thought.

"We're here," Eric said as the jet settled with a jerk on the runway in Ontario, California.

"Do you think we'll be able to recognize Aunt Sally from the picture Father gave us?" Susan asked anxiously as she tugged at her suitcase.

"How should I know?" Eric retorted. "Look at all these people."

"Let's just stand here and let her find us," Susan suggested.

Susan and Eric stopped. They scanned the faces of the people passing by.

"Hello. Hello, there!" a cheerful voice called out over the noisy, crowded room. "Eric? Susan?"

A woman wove her way through the crowd, waving her hand. Friendly, brown eyes peered from under a straw hat. She wore a pink flowered dress that made her cheeks look pink too. Eric and Susan just stared.

"Aunt Sally?" Eric said hesitantly.

"Young man, you've grown up, haven't you? And Susan! You look just like your mother." Her eyes looked sad for a moment; then she smiled and motioned for them to follow her.

Before long they located their baggage and Eric stuffed the suitcases into Aunt Sally's car. She waited for them to pile in, and then drove off toward the place that would be their new home.

"Here we are," she said stopping in front of a house that clung to a cliff overlooking the crashing waves of the Pacific Ocean.

Aunt Sally showed them to a room with twin beds. "I thought you might like to share this room tonight. It isn't easy to sleep in a new place. I have several empty rooms, and tomorrow you can each choose one. How does that sound?"

"Sure. Thank you, ma'am," Eric said.

"Aunt Sally, Father told us about the cliffs by the sea. He said you know all about the creatures that live in the tide pools and that they will teach us new things."

"That's right, Susan. Those sea creatures are certainly treasures. They taught me a lot. How to think differently, you might say."

Eric felt too tired to think about anything. He pulled the quilt up around his neck and soon fell asleep, but Susan's head danced with questions. Those sea creatures might teach her something interesting. They might teach her about God.

Discover the rest of the story of Eric and Susan. Read the whole series; **Treasures by the Sea, Octopus Encounter, Summer of the Sharks,** and **Intruder Alert!.**

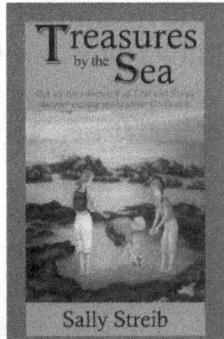

**Treasures** by the **Sea**

Sally Streib

Discover that sea shells, sea stars, and fish do more than slither, crawl, and swish. They teach you about a God that loves you.

**In Treasures by the Sea, you will learn lessons taught by:**
- Abalone shells that cling to rocks
- Seagulls that swallow hooks
- Moon snails that drill holes in their prey
- Fish that leap onto the beach
- Brittle stars that drop their arms
- Cowries that paint their own shells

**Discover answers to:**
- What happens when people die?
- What does it mean to forgive?
- How can you have victory over sin?
- How to accept Jesus in your heart.
- How to have strong faith.
- How to understand the Bible.
- How to know Jesus is coming again.
- What special gifts God gives everyone.

When twelve-year-old twins, Eric and Susan, move in with their aunt, they never dream that they will end up on a remote island paradise in the Bahamas for a coral reef restoration project! Susan bubbles over with excitement at the promise of underwater adventures. But the thought of cruising around in a large ocean, full of creepy and dangerous creatures, scares Eric. He tries to keep his fear a secret, and makes excuses for staying behind.

But with expert guidance from Aunt Sally and Uncle Merle, the twins are soon swimming, snorkeling, and SCUBA diving in a dazzling undersea world of wonder and beauty. The living kaleidoscope of swirling colors, light, and shapes teaches both scientific and spiritual lessons about the Creator lessons that draw Susan, Eric, and their friend, Kevin, closer to God.

Then one day, an encounter with a monster of the deep thrusts Eric face to face with his deepest fears and puts his faith to the test. Will Eric trust God to help him overcome his terror and keep him safe from harm?

**Octopus Encounter**

SALLY STREIB

Suddenly, something red hurtled right at Susan. Splat! It hit her mask and hung on. She struggled to her feet, screaming to her brother and jumping about. "Get it off! Get it off!"

"It's an octopus!" Eric screamed.

Come along with Susan, Eric, Aunt Sally and Uncle Merle on another underwater adventure. This time they're in Cayman. Susan is trying to discover her individual talents, interests, and spiritual gifts.

Until recently, the twins had always done everything together. But now Eric is going in a new direction—following his passion for underwater photography. Working with Mr. Wood at the Scripps Institute, Eric has been busy sorting, identifying, and enhancing the underwater photos he took on the previous trip to Eleuthera Island.

Susan wishes she had something that could make her feel as excited as Eric seems to be. She tried joining Eric at the institute, but discovered that trying to be like her brother isn't the answer. She will have to find her own consuming passion. But what will it be?

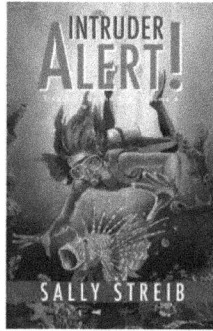

Suddenly, Susan felt Aunt Sally grab her shoulder. "What's wrong?" she said.

"That's a Lionfish. Don't touch it," Aunt Sally said. "Let's back off a few feet, lay quietly, and watch what happens next."

When an intruder threatens their beloved coral reefs, twins Eric and Susan jump at the chance to do their part to help. Together with Aunt Sally and Uncle Merle, their new adventure takes them from the shores of California, to Mexico, and then to the Caymen Islands.

Susan soon discovers that it is not only the coral reef that is in danger. God shows her that own life is in danger from a secret intruder. What can she do to defend herself?

Will Eric be able to help her break free? Can she use the secrets she learns in nature and the Bible to defend against the Intruder? With her family's help, Susan will discover God's plan to help identify and defend against the intruders in her life.

Join Eric and Susan on a new adventure as they dive into the wonderful world of God's creation and the Bible.

www.ingramcontent.com/pod-product-compliance
Lightning Source LLC
Chambersburg PA
CBHW072141270326
41931CB00010B/1844